MODERN PROPHETIC VOICES

MODERN PROPHETIC VOICES

FROM KIERKEGAARD TO BUCHMAN

R.C. MOWAT

NEW CHERWELL PRESS · OXFORD

First published in Great Britain 1994
by New Cherwell Press
7 Mount Street, Oxford OX2 6DH
Copyright © 1994 R.C. Mowat
British Library Cataloguing in Publication Data
Mowat, R.C.
Modern Prophetic Voices, from Kierkegaard to Buchman
1. Philosophy of Religion – Christianity
I. Title

ISBN 0-951-7695-4-5

Cover design by Jan Smith and photo by Alan Channer

Printed in Malta by Interprint

The world does not like people who try to make it a better place. Or rather it likes and admires them in theory, and from a distance ... hence humanity now, as of old, is busy making unpleasant the lives of the prophets that are with it, while celebrating the centenaries of their predecessors who are safely dead. To live constructively involves – to some men in small things, to others in large – unpopularity, hardship and sacrifice.

B.H. Streeter: *The Buddha and the Christ*

CONTENTS

page

Foreword   ii

Preface   iii

1. Perceptions   1

2. Perspectives   7

3. Philosophy   18

4. 'The greatest revolution'   23

5. The creative minority   38

6. International relations   44

7. Politics   52

8. Stages in world change   58

9. The family and education   65

10. Strategy   72

Biographical notes   81

FOREWORD

There are so many people I would like to thank for their help in making the production of this book possible, especially those who have come to the seminars, which we have held at Oxford every six weeks or so during the past year, to discuss the successive drafts. Some of these have contributed materially as well as morally to the project – my gratitude is no less if they are not named. Some are named in the references because of their contributions to the text; others, by telephone and letter, have helped to shape the text, avoid pitfalls, and have given warm encouragement. But to all those, whether named or not – especially those whose advice has not always been taken – as well as my son David, who designed the book and prepared it for publication, and my wife Renée for constant support, and hospitality for the seminars, I wish to express my warmest thanks. I would also like to thank Lord Rees-Mogg for permission to include part of his article which appeared in *The Times*.

It will be noticed that I have plagiarised myself, sometimes quite substantially, in quotations from previous books, *Decline and Renewal* and *Creating the European Community*. I apologise to those who may take exception to repetitions of what they previously have read.

R.C.M.

PREFACE

Where to place Frank Buchman among those who have spoken with prophetic voices during the last two centuries about the future of civilisation? Some of these — Kierkegaard, Lincoln, Streeter, Schweitzer, Schuman — were Christians (the list is not of course exhaustive). Some were historians: Thomas Arnold (father of Matthew) could be added to Burckhardt and others who foresaw decline like that of Greece and Rome. Others, like Lecky, pinned their hopes on the progress of technology as promising a bright future. In Buchman's case his calling was to 'remake the world' by bringing change to men and nations.

Lincoln and Schuman were statesmen of the first order, who not only salvaged something from catastrophe, but began to build anew. Buchman, in the tradition of the ancient Hebrew prophets, influenced and encouraged Schuman, Adenauer and other statesmen and rulers. Like the prophets, he was also challenging people in general, predicting disaster if there was not moral change. In so doing he extended the scope and scale of the Anglo-American campus movement which, under men like Moody, Drummond and Mott, had — into the early years of this century — brought unnumbered younger people to a Christian calling and commitment. Buchman's concern continued to be for the younger generation, but he reached those of all ages, and indeed of all faiths — or none. In so doing he transcended his predecessors, moving in a different dimension with far-seeing strategic aims. Others in India, China or elsewhere ran missionary campaigns, but Buchman became the friend of Gandhi, Sun Yat-sen and Viscount Shibusawa, as well as of crowned heads, trade union leaders and statesmen in Europe, not to mention his range of friends in all walks of life in America.

What began as a spontaneously formed group around Buchman inevitably became – as numbers increased to hundreds and thousands – a movement with a name and a structure. This development demands separate treatment, as do the political and economic consequences of his work and of the statesmen whom he influenced. Though, for instance, Tunisia and Morocco appear in this context in *Remaking the World* (the annotated record of his speeches), this aspect of his work is not discussed in the following pages, nor has there been space to consider the outcome in situations like that of France and Germany in the aftermath of the war later than the initial resolution of the conflict.

Similarly in industry, the impact of Frank Buchman's work in improving labour relations in many situations in Europe, the American hemisphere, Australia and India, has not been touched on, nor (in regard to the economies of particular countries) its contribution to the postwar 'miracles' in Germany, Japan and France. In social matters, for instance in curbing alcoholism by way of Alcoholics Anonymous, the reader must look elsewhere.[1]

The question may arise as to how far predictions and warnings, or even examples of change, which date back to the early or middle part of the century can be valid today, since another half century of revolutions and transformations, political, social and technological, has passed, and these changes continue to happen at astounding speed. But if civilisation was apparently 'at stake'[2] in the 1930s (though surviving the second World War) its future still remains precarious – even as does 'the long-term existence of the human race itself', according to Paul Kennedy.[3] In the face of powerful 'forces which are changing the world,' the need, he writes, is for 'new thinking, new structures'[4] if the 'steady and insidious decline'[5] of the USA and most other countries and continents is to be arrested, let alone reversed. Within the USA, as elsewhere, and between the better-off and less advantaged parts of the planet, the rich are getting richer and the poor poorer. Greed, rather than need, is rapidly destroying the environment. Vast areas are becoming derelict. The USA will have to be 'a different kind of country'[6] if it is to set a pattern and give the leadership required, and this applies to those other countries in the well-to-do bracket.

As fresh perspectives develop, so does the work in recent years of many besides historians – scientists, mathematicians, economists and sociologists have all contributed to making fresh interpretations of the past and predictions for the future. The barriers between science and religion have been falling as researchers give their minds to probing the mysteries of existence and of life. For the mystery and miracle remain. No longer is it possible to do without the hypothesis of an infinite and omnipresent factor, constantly creating forms and structures in the midst of dissolution and decay, with an apparent aim of increasing complexity and abundance (though with occasional extinctions). Since purpose cannot be conceived except as a function of personality, 'God' continues to be the name of this Being in the Western version of our Abrahamic tradition.

A vast bibliography might follow. I recommend as a start Garth Lean: *Frank Buchman — a Life* (London 1985; in USA under the title *On the Tail of a Comet*, 1988) and M. Mitchell Waldrop: *Complexity* (London 1993); also my *Decline and Renewal: Europe Ancient and Modern* (New Cherwell Press, Oxford 1991), which contains an adequate bibliography.

References

In these notes, and in those at the end of each chapter, certain references may be abbreviated, as follows:

FB: Frank Buchman: *Remaking the World* (London 1961)
BHS: B.H. Streeter: *The God Who Speaks* (London 1943)
RCM: R.C. Mowat: *Decline and Renewal: Europe Ancient and Modern* (Oxford 1991)

1. Dick B.: *The Oxford Group and Alcoholics Anonymous* (Glen Abbey Books, USA, 1992)

2. FB: 105, USA, 27/8/39

3. Paul Kennedy: *Preparing for the Twenty-first Century* (London 1993), 330

4. Ibid., 288

5. Ibid., 311

6. Ibid., 324

CHAPTER 1

PERCEPTIONS

Our generation is living in the critical period when decisions concerning the fate of mankind have to be made. Do we continue wars, with the danger of nuclear annihilation? Do we continue to develop the consumer society for a privileged minority worldwide, threatening the habitat by pollution and the squandering of resources, while the majority of mankind – burdened by debt and by armaments they cannot afford – sink unto utter destitution, a prey to famines and epidemics? Or do we try to change the mode of life fundamentally, and so help to ensure a future for our descendants? The signs are clear as to the way in which the extinction of the species (humanity) could take place, by self-destruction – unless there is change.

By the middle of the last century doubts about the future of European civilisation were becoming evident. The pessimism of the Danish philosopher Søren Kierkegaard went to the extreme limit. He had no faith that Christianity could be a dynamic force to rejuvenate society – from the earliest times, in his view, it had been watered down to become merely an anodyne to keep people comfortable in their worldly lives. 'The history of Christendom is the history of the subtle discarding of Christianity.'[1] The only hope was in 'the single man' who could make the leap of enthusiasm by deciding to follow closely 'the Model', Jesus, ready 'to stand alone, forsaken, scorned and ridiculed.'[2] He could then 'serve in suffering and help indirectly',[3] but even so would have little effect on an evil and sinful world which had fallen away from God.

'I understood perfectly well', he wrote, 'that I could not possibly succeed in taking the comfortable and secure *via media* in which most people pass their lives. I had either to throw myself into perdition and sensuality, or to choose the religious way absolutely as the only thing.' He broke off his engagement to his fiancée, and as a single man, in both senses, he followed his prophetic calling. But he knew that his message would be ignored, and catastrophe would result.

Imagine a very great ship, greater, if you will, than the biggest ships we have at present; suppose it has room for 1,000 passengers, and of course it is equipped on the greatest possible scale with conveniences, comforts, luxuries, etc. It is towards night. In the cabin they are having a merry time, everything illuminated in the most resplendent way, everything glitters. In short all is merriment and good cheer ... and the merriest of all is the captain.

The white speck is there in the horizon; it will be a dreadful night. But no one sees the white speck or divines what it means. But there is one that sees it and knows what it means — but he is a passenger. He has no command on the ship and is unable to do anything decisive. However, to do the only thing in his power, he sends a message to the captain to come on deck for an instant. There is considerable delay; finally he comes out but will listen to nothing, and with a jest he hastens down to the noise and reckless joy of the society in the cabin, where the captain's health is drunk and he responds complacently. In his anguish the poor passenger ventures out once more to disturb the captain; but now the captain has even become discourteous to him. Nevertheless the speck in the horizon remains unchanged – 'It will be a dreadful night.'[4]

Even though, for Kierkegaard, human society had always been the same, given over to the power of evil, he recognised a certain falling off from the creative energy and passion of the previous age which had culminated in the French Revolution. 'A revolutionary age is an age of action; ours is the age of advertisement and publicity.'

Nietzsche a few years later had no doubts that decadence had already overtaken Europe. Culture was being 'uprooted in the increasing rush of life, and the decay of all reflection and simplicity ... The nations are drawing away in enmity again and long to tear each other to pieces.'[5]

Nietzsche was lecturing at Basel (Basle) in Switzerland at the same time as Jakob Burckhardt, who made his name with a classic of the 1860's, *The Civilisation of the Renaissance in Italy*.

For the illusions of 'progress ... the merciless optimism which is springing up everywhere,' Burckhardt cast the principal blame on Rousseau as one of the chief inspirers of the French Revolution 'with his doctrine of the goodness of human nature.' By the 1870's 'the idea of the natural goodness of man had turned, among the intelligent strata of Europe, into the idea of progress, i.e. undisturbed money-making and modern comforts, with philanthropy as a sop to conscience ... The only conceivable salvation would be for this insane optimism, in great and small, to disappear from people's brains.'

People do not like to imagine a world whose rulers utterly ignore law ... and who would rule with utter brutality. But these are the people into whose hands the world is being driven by the competition among all parties for the participation of the masses on any and every question.[6]

The most he could hope for was 'a few half-hearted decades, a sort of Roman Empire,' assailed by the kind of pessimism which became 'a generally recognised attitude in the third and fourth centuries.' He saw the Franco-Prussian War of 1870-1 as initiating an era of wars, to be ended perhaps by 'a great war, with the resulting lasting peace. But what a horrible price to pay! ... The final end might well be an Imperium Romanum (only when we are dead, to be sure).' He foresaw the military state which will have to turn 'industrialist, with its mounds of men in the yards and factories', for whom 'a planned degree of poverty' would be necessary, 'with promotions and uniforms.' Germany would only survive if 'something great, new and liberating' could arise – 'it will have to have its martyrs'. As for Russia, it would be 'reduced to confusion by acts of violence ... sheer, unlimited violence.'

In France Pierre Joseph Proudhon wrote in 1860: 'Old Europe is rushing towards ruin,'

Immorality and scepticism are competing to destroy society ... What a downfall it is for France, particularly after a revolution like 1789. We have gone right back to the rule of the sword, the bondage of nations, to unprincipled living and orgies! ... Our nation has been in a state of decadence for 30 years ... I foresee nothing but more decadence if I judge the future by the false ideas that are currently held in France and shared by so many honest citizens.[7]

Max Nordau could claim a wider European view than others whose lives had been largely passed in their own countries. He was a Hungarian Jew, strongly influenced in his student days by his Italian professor. He spent many years in Paris, was deeply familiar with English literature, and wrote in German. His book *Degeneration* appeared in 1892-3.

He defines decadence as 'a practical emancipation from traditional discipline ... the trampling underfoot of all barriers which enclose brutal greed of lucre and lust of pleasure ... the shameless ascendancy of base impulses and motives, which were, if not virtuously suppressed, at least hypocritically hidden ... the vanishing of ideals in art, and no more power in its accepted forms to arouse emotion ... The end of an established order, which for thousands of years has satisfied logic, fettered depravity, and in every art matured something of beauty.'[8]

A contemporary voice is that of Solzhenitsyn, writing in 1973, some sixteen years before the collapse of the Soviet Union. He points to 'the multiple impasse in which Western civilisation (which Russia long ago chose the honour of belonging to) finds itself.'

> All that 'endless progress' turned out to be an insane, ill-considered, furious dash into a blind alley. A civilisation greedy for 'perpetual progress' has now choked and is on its last legs. And it is not 'convergence' that faces us and the western world now, but total renewal and reconstruction in both East and West, for both are in the same impasse.
> Bearing in mind the state of the people's morals, their

spiritual condition and their relationships with one another and with society, all the *material* achievements we trumpet so loudly are petty and worthless ... The considerations which guide our country must be these: to encourage the *inner*, the moral, the healthy development of the people ... I myself see Christianity today as the only living spiritual force capable of undertaking the spiritual healing of Russia. But I request and propose no special privileges for it.[9]

References

1. Søren Kierkegaard: *The Last Years: Journals 1853-55* (Ed. R. Gregor Smith, (Glasgow 1965), 63

2. ibid., 354-5

3. Søren Kierkegaard: *The Present Age* (Ed. A. Dru, Glasgow 1962), 96

4. Walter Lowrie: *A Short Life of Kierkegaard* (Princeton 1965), 147, 231-2

5. Crane Brinton: *Nietzsche* (New York 1965), 107

6. Jakob Burckhardt: *Letters* (London 1955), 170, 147, 207, 107, 143, 211, 151, 202

7. P.J. Proudhon: *Selected Writings* (London 1969); Letter, 3/5/1860, p.197, and 12/10/1861, 220-22

8. Max Nordau: *Degeneration* (English translation, London 1895), 5

9. Alexander Solzhenitsyn: *Letter to Soviet Leaders* (tr. H. Sternberg, London 1974), 20, 21, 35, 55, 56.

CHAPTER 2

PERSPECTIVES

Oxford in the 1930's was not without prophetic voices. One of those who commanded attention was Burnett Hillman Streeter, Provost of Queen's College and a Canon of Hereford Cathedral. He was among the foremost biblical scholars of his day, with a world-wide reputation as a philosopher. When a young man at Oxford, he had won his way from agnosticism to a robust faith. But after a while he realised that his position 'was very far from being intellectually water-tight,' and he set forth again on his quest, buoyed up by the 'reinvigorating inspiration of the Summer Conferences of the Student Christian Movement' (1905).[1] After 'long and repeated discussion' with philosophers and scientists 'as well as theologians of many Christian denominations, and students or adherents of the great religions of the East', he expressed his findings by way of group discussions in jointly written books which marked a new era in religious thought.

In his search for Truth (which he wrote with a capital T) and his expression of it, he had at one time so offended his congregation that they took to their feet as he mounted the pulpit in the cathedral. He had been threatened with deprivation of his Orders. But eventually 'the Church of England had quietly adjusted itself to his views and christened him respectable.'[2]

He early perceived that philosophers and theologians, including himself, had been asking the wrong questions, whether religion – in this case Christianity – was true, and how to explain the existence of evil. The real question was not 'the problem of evil' but 'the problem of good'.[3]

> Death could not exist unless there were life, nor disease if there were no such thing as health ... Good might exist without evil, evil could not exist without good; for evil is either a parody of, or an obstacle to, good ... If good is more positive and more fundamental than evil, the existence of the good is the thing which most needs to be accounted for.

When considering the prospects for civilisation in the thirties he, like Kierkegaard, used a liner as a parable.

> Our world is like an Atlantic liner deprived of rudder, compass, sextant, charts, and wireless tackle, yet compelled to go full steam ahead. There is magnificence, comfort, pulsating power; but whither are we going? Does that depend solely on the accident of circumstances and the ever-changing balance of conflicting interests and ambitions? Or is there available for man, if he so will, guidance on his dark and dangerous course from some Wisdom higher than his own?[4]

Streeter's answer, developed in his last book *The God Who Speaks*, was in the affirmative. Evidently, in his view, belief in God is basic. From that belief it follows 'that the Universe is not the product of blind chance, but is controlled by purpose,' for (he goes on) 'it is a contradiction in terms to say that God exists but has no plan. And to say that His plan can only contemplate the big outline and not also minor detail, is to reduce His intelligence to the scale of ours.'[5]

> He must have a plan – not only for the Universe or for this planet, but also for each nation, each city, every business,

every family, every individual. It is not necessarily a static and wholly inelastic plan, as the classical doctrine of Predestination would suggest; it may well be one which, like the plan of a general staff, is not only capable of, but is designed for, modification as the course of battle develops. But we must affirm that the Divine Intelligence cannot be content with something less full of purpose and precision than what a human general or statesman would call a 'plan' ...[6]

At this point someone will say, how am I to know God's plan? There is no need, I would reply, to know the whole of God's plan. All I need to know is His plan for *me*. Nor do I need to know the details of that plan for my whole future or even for a year ahead. It is enough to know it day by day.[7]

But there is a condition for becoming aware of His plan – putting right any known wrong in our life. If we do this, experience shows that the 'still small voice' of 'the Beyond that is within' will tell us the next thing that God wishes us to do. It may be to right some other wrong; it may be to do some positive piece of service; it may be a 'happy thought' in regard to some work or project; it may be an untried approach in some personal relationship; it may be a flash of insight into new truth.[8]

God's plan assuredly aims at harmony, not chaos; and in human affairs self-centredness, dishonesty, rancour, and the like inevitably produce chaos. Knowledge of God's plan must, therefore, be ethically conditioned. Thus there is an inner coherence between the conception of God's plan and the two convictions – that conscience is 'the voice of God', and that certain intuitions, which come to the individual with an imperative quality, may be interpreted as 'divine guidance'. Certainly, no individual can claim infallibility either for the dictates of his own conscience or for his own conviction of guidance; to do that would be to disregard, not only the frailty

9

of human nature and its capacity for self-deception, but also the limitation of the individual mind by the social environment in which it has been formed. Nevertheless, without some such communication – however limited by human infirmities – between the human and the divine, it is hard to see how God could direct and educate a world of free and conscious souls.[9]

Despite his pessimism about the future of civilisation, Kierkegaard also believed that God could communicate with individuals.

The 'immediate' person thinks and imagines that when he prays, the important thing, the thing he must concentrate upon is that *God should hear* what HE *is praying for*. Yet in the true, eternal sense it is just the reverse: the true relation in prayer is not when God hears what is prayed for, but when *the person praying* continues to pray until he is *the one who hears*, who hears what God wills. The 'immediate' person, therefore, uses many words, and, therefore, makes demands in his prayers; the true man of prayer only *attends*.[10]

For Streeter, on this possibility of communication between God and man the future of civilisation depends – as long as the resulting *change* in the individual goes deep enough. 'In the last resort, the battle for "the salvaging of civilisation" must be fought out on the plane of the psychology of the individual man and woman.'[11] As for Christianity – if it 'is to save our threatened civilisation, its representatives must deflect their interest from theological discussion and denominational rivalries to a practical dealing with those basic infirmities of human nature which are the tap-root of all human ills.'[12]

When Streeter wrote these words the threat that was looming was the second World War. This, it was feared, might so shake the foundations of civilised life that mankind might regress to a dark age. Since then the threats have become more specific, not only to the sophisticated modes of living in the 'developed' countries, but to the habitat itself. In addition to pollution, global warming, destruction of forests and of the ozone layer, overpopulation has now reached the point where food production is no longer keeping up with the increase of human beings.

Civilisation survived – at a cost which cannot be calculated. But as the millennium moves towards its end, dire forecasts are being made: it might be the twilight of a long phase of world history – 'the underlying conditions that precipitated the great explosion of modern progress may themselves be coming to an end. A millennium that has witnessed ever-accelerating technical change seems destined to end in dramatic fashion.'[13]

Our view should certainly stretch back over the millennium if we want to understand what is happening now. But beyond that, new approaches to history, by way of the geological record and evolution of species, suggest further perceptions which could bring greater clarity.

Mankind appeared after many million years of species evolution, while life itself had only begun following vast ages of geological change. The evolution of species seems to have occurred, not gradually, but in bursts when a multitude of creatures appeared, followed by periods when such species were greatly reduced – or

11

even extinguished, like the dinosaurs. The survival of the fittest was one mechanism whereby both the development and reductions occurred. Those species which could cope with certain conditions survived and multiplied, while others disappeared.[14]

Are such principles also apparent in the evolution of mankind? Various types of hominids appeared in different parts of the world. Some of these, notably in Africa, began to spread across the globe. Some, like Neanderthal Man, disappeared, or were merged in more 'successful' types. Eventually the norm of homo sapiens was established world-wide.

So with civilisation, once our nomadic forebears settled down to agriculture, building villages and eventually cities. At the beginning, some 7,000 years ago, civilisation appeared as a few scattered patches around the globe. These gradually linked up as trade brought them into communication with each other. After more millennia civilisation appeared world-wide. Now it has become the norm of mankind's social life. The few tribes surviving with Stone Age techniques are regarded as curiosities, in danger of reduction and extinction – or of being 'civilised'.

A process in the history of the planet is observable, from gaseous to geological forms, eventually making life possible, and by way of ever more complex types of marine and terrestrial life, to the primates and eventually Man. But cataclysms and extinctions indicate that this process, continuous in the long term, moves discontinuously in the shorter term. The record of species evolution, with its apparent bursts of creation, followed by reductions and

12

extinctions, is matched in the history of civilisation by a similar cyclical element – the rise and fall of specific civilisations, with a long-term but also cyclical development of arts, crafts and technology, of mathematics and science, and of awareness and understanding of the physical and metaphysical environment.

In our Western civilisation (I write as a Westerner), the comparative study of various civilisations brought forth works like Spengler's *Decline of the West* and Toynbee's *Study of History*. These summed up much that had already been written as far back as the mid-19th century about the oncoming decadence of the West, that is the abandonment, by a substantial minority, of norms and standards in manners and morals, and their almost wholesale rejection in the arts and literature and 'the media' new and old. 'Artists, philosophers and scientists were nibbling and hacking away at the absolute standards of the old confident West.'[15]

What is the future of civilisation in the face of declining moral standards, along with the nuclear threat and environmental degradation? Even before the second world war, movements aiming at the renewal of nations and society had taken over in Russia, Italy and Germany. But the 'isms' – Communism, Fascism, Nazism and their imitators – ignored the moral foundations on which such renewal had to be based. Though sharing in the spiritual upsurge that (with its cycles of intensity and diminution) had been evident since the Renaissance, these movements perverted the aspirations of multitudes for a better life – they failed to deliver the promised good life except briefly and for a privileged few, and fell into ways

13

which were clearly evil and disastrous for millions.

For years the 'enemy' of the West was embodied in the Communist empire. Now the perception once more shifts back to the eternal truth that the line between good and evil passes through every human heart. The issue appears to be much clearer now – whether secular materialism will dominate or whether the next age will be a spiritual one.[16]

The troubled history of the interwar years demonstrated once again the need to observe the moral guidelines for personal and social life enunciated by sages and saints, and by prophets and founders of faiths, since the awakening awareness of Man in the early phases of civilisation. The Hebrew prophets expressed perceptions both for the short-term and the long; the short-term, for instance, regarding the exile in Babylon and the long-term for millennia ahead. There is an almost uncanny realism in the lurid pictures they paint of a period of something like nuclear war or 'Chernobyls', with a movement by mankind to get rid of the weapons of war, turning them into the equivalent of farm tractors and harvesters. At that future phase of history 'they will not teach war any more' – no more sales expeditions and exhibitions of armaments and how to use them.

'It would seem,' says Streeter,

that it must also be part of God's plan to 'raise up' from time to time individuals of exceptional insight, whose words or actions may serve to provide more ordinary persons both with a criterion of value and a stimulus to progress. In other words, there is an inner coherence between the belief that God has a plan for mankind and the fact of the emergence in history of the exceptional individuals to whom we give the name of 'prophets'[17] ... If we say that the prophet has evolved out of the soothsayer, we must insist that it is a case of what has been styled 'emergent evolution', that is to say, there has come into existence a new kind ...[18]

God, so far as we can see, operates in accordance with large uniformities that we name the laws of Nature, which include the laws of human psychology so far as such exist. Suppose, then, He does at times act in some special way upon the consciousness of any individual, we should expect this action, not to supersede, but to stimulate his highest powers, and to result in an enhancement of his profoundest insights. At such moments the individual might rise far above the level at which ordinarily either he or his contemporaries live and think ...[19]

The insistence [by the Hebrew prophets] on the centrality of ethics to religion prepared the way for the recognition of religion as an individual as well as a social matter[20]... They are not the spokesmen of tradition, they are the leaders in a revolution[21]...That insistence on an indissoluble connection between religion and ethics is a relatively rare achievement.[22]

Frank Buchman, the initiator of the Oxford Group of the 1920's and 30's, had much in common with Streeter, who became his friend. He too was steeped in the words and wisdom of the Hebrew prophets.

You remember Amos, speaking of a famine abroad in the land, declared it was not a famine of water or of bread, but a famine of hearing the words of the Lord ... This same famine is afflicting the world today ... A situation is growing up in which people will want God to speak to them.[23]

In practical terms 'what does it mean to listen to guidance?'

15

The prophets of old knew. They listened and they gave their rulers specific direction in national and foreign affairs. They warned about treaties. They warned about invasions. They gave the rulers insight to anticipate disaster.[24]

The historic basis of nationhood [as] stated ... by the prophets of old ... has withstood the test of centuries. The prophet Isaiah says, 'And all thy children shall be taught of the Lord and great shall be the peace of thy children ... Nations that knew not thee shall run unto thee because of the Lord thy God' ... British labour leaders sent a message to the American capital with these words, 'We need men who will make real the vision of the prophet Micah.'[25]

Read the seventh chapter of Jeremiah, starting at the twenty-third verse. He is a prophet with a message for modern people. Begin with the seventh chapter, and then study the whole, because you have to have in your mind a framework for the rebuilding of a nation.

'Hearken unto My voice and ye shall be My people; and walk ye in the way that I command you, that it may be well with you.'[26]

References

1. B.H. Streeter: *Reality* (London, 1927), viii

2. Alan Thornhill: *One Fight More* (London 1943), 28

3. *Reality*, 222

4. B.H. Streeter: *The God Who Speaks* (London 1936), 3

5. BHS: 10

6. BHS: 11

7. BHS: 13

8. BHS: 14

9. BHS: 15

10. *The Journals of Kierkegaard, 1834-1854* (ed. Alexander Dru, Glasgow 1958), 97

11. BHS: 134

12. BHS: 135

13. J. Dale Davidson & William Rees-Mogg: *The Great Reckoning* (London 1992), 15

14. David M. Raup: *Extinction: Bad Genes or Bad Luck?* (New York/London 1991)

15. J.M. Roberts: *The Triumph of the West* (London 1985), 11

16. John Lester (letter)

17. BHS: 15

18. BHS: 26

19. BHS: 42

20. BHS: 33

21. BHS: 140

22. BHS: 140

23. FB: 36, Philadelphia, 19/6/36; 107, USA, 29/10/39

24. FB: 130, USA, 4/6/40

25. FB: 112, 29/10/39; Micah 4: 1-5

26. FB: 8, Oslo, March 1935

CHAPTER 3

PHILOSOPHY

For Streeter, tracking down truth about the universe and God was a lifetime's 'adventure' (the title of one of his books). Pursuing the 'two parallel avenues', science and religion, he made it clear that 'religion' and the Christian religion are by no means identical terms. So came his Bampton Lectures of 1932, published under the title *The Buddha and the Christ*. These were not intended as a study in comparative religion, but to 'throw light on the character of the Unseen Power behind the Universe', and so 'provide the basis of a working philosophy for everyday life.'[1]

A world philosophy has to take over, a 'mind-set', to use modern jargon, whereby the world's millions will resort to the modes of discussion and the will for harmony and concern for the other parties or people which characterise democracy at its best. Buchman spoke of a '*world* philosophy' because such changes in today's world are inconceivable unless on a global scale. 'A new world philosophy is needed, a world philosophy capable of creating a new era of constructive relationships between men and nations ... We need a whole new content and conception of life ... This world philosophy will emerge as people begin to get their direction from the living God.'[2]

A world philosophy – it recalls Vera Brittain's cry from the heart after visiting Germany in 1924, humiliated and impoverished as it was after the first World War.

> How much there was to be done for this suffering Europe, this stricken humanity; we could not, even if we would, leave it to its agony and live in the past! To find some guiding principle of action, some philosophy of life, some constructive hope upon whose wings this crippled age might swing forward into a fairer future – that at least remained and always would remain, for us who had experienced in our own souls those incalculable depths into which Germany had fallen.[3]

After the second World War – with France and Germany this time achieving reconciliation and partnership – Europe can (and must, in Paul Kennedy's view) move forward to 'new thinking and new structures'.[4]

In Buchman's words,

> A nation's thinking is in ruins before a nation is in ruins ... The one thing we really need is to be guided by God's Holy Spirit. That is the Force we ought to study ... The Holy Spirit will teach us how to think and live.[5]

Besides Buchman's, another voice was raised in the inter-war period, saying that the decay of civilisation could only be reversed by the renewal of its ethical basis. Emerging like some Old Testament prophet from his hospital in the rain-forest of West Africa, Albert Schweitzer gave a powerful series of lectures at Oxford on 'the decay and restoration of civilisation'.

> If the ethical is the essential element in civilisation, decadence changes into renaissance as soon as ethical activities are set to work again in our convictions and in the ideas which we undertake to stamp upon reality ... The only conceivable way of bringing about a reconstruction of our world on new lines

19

is first of all to become new men ourselves ... The difficult problems with which we have to deal, even those which lie entirely in the material and economic sphere, are in the last resort only to be solved by an inner change of character ... Civilisation can only revive when there shall come into being in a number of individuals a new tone of mind independent of the one prevalent among the crowd and in opposition to it, a tone of mind which will gradually win influence over the collective one, and in the end determine its character.[6]

Buchman was saying much the same thing as Schweitzer, but whereas Schweitzer had polite acclaim from those who paid attention, Buchman encountered opposition. Many, it is true, accepted his message, but others denounced him. It was the same experience as that of the ancient prophets and the founders of the great faiths. As he said, 'persecution is the fire that forges prophets.'[7] The reason was that whereas Schweitzer expressed his truth in generalities, Buchman dealt in specifics.

God can put thoughts into your mind. Have you ever listened for them? Have you ever tried taking pencil and paper, and writing down the thoughts that come to you? They may look like ordinary thoughts. But be honest about them. You might get a new picture of yourself. Absolute honesty, absolute purity, absolute unselfishness, absolute love. Those are Christ's standards. Are they yours? You may have to put things straight. I had to. I began by writing to six people, admitting that ill-will between us was my fault, and not theirs. Then I could really help people. Remember – if you want the world to get straight, get straight yourself.[8]

Another prophetic figure, Laurens van der Post, makes the same point.

We have got to remake ourselves first. Until we have dealt with error in ourselves we cannot properly deal with what is wrong in the world.[9]

This is what actually happened in the 'Hellenistic' Age during the decline of the Greco-Roman civilisation. A momentous mind-change took place – because enough ordinary people (as well as some of the best educated) began to apply absolute standards to their lives. This was in part due to the coming of Christianity, but also to Stoicism (not just as a philosophy, but for some a noble and exacting faith) as well as to other religions from the Orient, notably Judaism and Zoroastrianism. It was a turning away from out-moded beliefs in gods and goddesses who behaved all too much like humans, towards belief in the One God, transcendent in majesty but immanent, in a personal sense, in humanity – the Saviour God promising eternal life: a movement throughout the Roman world, predating the triumph of Christianity. A new 'philosophy' was taking over hearts and minds on a scale which made the political leaders of the day take notice, and in the case of the greatest of them, Constantine I, led to his giving a privileged position in the Empire to the Christian Church, with generous and constant support. Two and a half centuries later the Rome of Gregory the Great was totally different from the Rome of the Caesars.

We are entitled to hope that a similar evolution may now be on the way.

'Hope, for many believers, means the hope of a happy issue to some personal trial, such as the recovery from illness, or the expectation that beyond this life they may ultimately reach heaven. But it must also look to the working out of God's purpose on earth. Such hope is not a luxury, an extra granted to a few bold spirits, but necessary equipment for every son and daughter of Abraham. It is a gift of God freely offered, but we have to choose between it and messing about in smaller concerns — my success, my project, even my comfort.'[10]

References

1. *Reality*, 222ff, vii. *The Buddha and the Christ* (London 1932), ix

2. FB: 107, 108, 112, 114; USA 29/10/39

3. Vera Brittain: *Testament of Youth* (London 1978), 645

4. Kennedy, 288

5. FB: 145, Mackinac, July 1943

6. A. Schweitzer: *The Decay and the Restoration of Civilization* (London 1932), 64, 60, 73

7. FB: 81, London, November 1938

8. FB: FB, 40, London, 9/8/36

9. Laurens van der Post: *Walk with a White Bushman* (Harmondsworth 1986), 112

10. Michael Hutchinson (letter to author)

CHAPTER 4

'THE GREATEST REVOLUTION'

Such a change as happened in Antiquity was a revolution. The change which must happen worldwide today, if civilisation is to survive, will have to be a revolution as great or greater. The need is for a different type of revolutionary from those who manned the barricades or shot their way to power. Whatever we do is only part of the process: we have to leave the main part to the Power that causes the seed to grow. It has to be a 'revolution of silence'.

What the prophets of old were proclaiming, says one of their modern representatives, André Chouraqui, was not 'progress', but a mutation – a total revolution in society. If we can envision such a change in human relations on a world scale, we must still admit that we are in a preparatory phase when the challenge is to personal change in our character and motives, and so come nearer that level of living which he expresses as 'transparent towards God and men, cleansed of all dirt so that the light coming from on high can penetrate and illuminate us.'[1]

In a recent interview he speaks of St Paul's aspiration to

reconcile Israel with the nations of the world. He genuinely believed that to achieve this would be to secure the Kingdom of Heaven among us. But this vision, utopian and mystic, has today become an urgent historical imperative. Reconcile the Jews, the Christians and the Muslims around the focal point of Jerusalem, and you create a community of two billion

23

people extending over five continents, united by the same faith, the same ideals, and a unique spiritual power.[2]

Chouraqui's conviction is that silence should forge regenerated humanity.

> We must be the midwives of the new world which must be born ... We must found a new order whose roots would reach down into the still living depths of Israel, Christianity and Islam. The nearer we get back to our sources, the nearer we will be to each other, without ceasing to be intensely ourselves ... I am expecting men who will arise, fully attentive to silence, and ready at the zero hour of humanity.[3]

Dr Charis Waddy writes:

> Buchman had the sense of such a 'zero hour for humanity' as he set off for Europe in 1946. If his vision of a world remade was to be fulfilled, the greatest and most urgent need for change was in the shattered heartlands of Christian civilisation. The traditionally Christian nations had so deteriorated in their living that they had involved the whole world in two wars and a spiral of poverty and pollution. If they were to make a fresh start, they owed it to the rest of humanity to put into practice the message of repentance, cleansing and forgiveness they had betrayed. To the group he took with him, to enter Britain, France and Germany, he spoke of the best in Western civilisation. They were 'in a global effort to win the world to our Lord and Saviour Jesus Christ. The great truths of the Gospel will once more become great. It is the whole message of the Gospel of Our Lord and Saviour Jesus Christ.'[4]
>
> Earlier, speaking of the meaning of revolution, he had pointed out that accepting Christ's standards, listening to God and obeying are steps on the road to revolution. The Cross of

Christ should never be regarded as a mere symbol or dogma but a deep challenge to change. 'If we obey what we hear, it is conceivable that together we will usher in the greatest revolution of all time, whereby the Cross of Christ will transform the world.'[5]

The clue to understanding this statement of Buchman's revolutionary aims lies in 'the great truths of the Gospel' as enunciated by Jesus himself. Answering a question from one of the scribes, Jesus said: 'The first of all the commandments is: The Lord our God is one Lord; and thou shalt love the Lord thy God with all thy heart, and with all thy soul, and with all thy mind, and with all thy strength: this is the first commandment. And the second is like, namely this, Thou shalt love thy neighbour as thyself. There is none other commandment greater than these.'[6]

A recent statement in the London *Times*[7] by Lord Rees-Mogg reminds its readers that the spiritual inspiration through faith 'flows in loving actions towards other people.' Christians see in Jesus 'a perfect identity' between that which is inner and spiritual – 'the divine spirit', as the writer calls it – and the 'outward life of action'. But he goes on to say that 'all the world's religions express this relationship in their own way', and reinforces his point, that it is the loving actions which count in a life of prayer, with the words of the aged Apostle John whose last sermon was simply 'little children, love one another'. For, he says, 'this is also the aim of the Jewish religion, of Islam, of Buddhism, particularly in the high form of Tibetan Buddhism, of Sikhism and of contemplative Hinduism. In this sense at least, all the religions have a common purpose and may be compared to different telescopes which look up at the same night sky. No doubt the telescopes are different; some may be more powerful or better focused than others. If human beings are in touch with what Buddhists would call 'the wisdom mind' and Christians the Holy Spirit — the two concepts are not doctrinally identical — they will be naturally impelled to good deeds.'

Mahatma Gandhi's experience was (in his words):

> As my contact with real Christians, that is men living in fear of God, increased, I saw the Sermon on the Mount was the whole Christianity for him who wanted to live a Christian life. It is that sermon which endeared Jesus to me.

He was asked, 'What is the most effective way of preaching the Gospel of Christ?' to which he replied:

> To live the gospel is the most effective way — most effective in the beginning, in the middle and in the end ... But I love those who never preach, but live the life according to their lights. If therefore you go on serving people and ask them also to serve they would understand.[8]

These words are borne out in Buchman's speeches, quoting leaders of various faiths, as well as their scriptures. He quotes Isaiah as typifying 'the pristine contribution' of Judaism,[9] and refers to a statement by the Rector of El Azhar University at Cairo, that Buchman's work was 'to spread the principles of peace, love and sound morals without individual and national differences. We ourselves will co-operate to establish this sound, God-inspired ideology.'[10] Buchman tells how Premier U Nu 'expressed his gratitude for the new direction given by this ideology to the students of Burma.'[11] Numerous references to India, Pakistan, China and Japan make the same point.

> Frank Buchman was so vividly alive that he kindled hope, which made it worthwhile for the cynical and despairing to face the necessary changes, that is to face sin and evil. His message was uncompromisingly Christian – there was never any doubt about that. He constantly shared his own message of change, but with the delicacy, the restraint, the sensitiveness to the man or nation he was addressing, with which he constantly re-expressed the profound truths of the Cross. He did not face them with a dogma but with an experience. His work cannot be understood without addressing the controversial paradox: men and women of other traditions of faith felt drawn to work with him – perhaps *because* he was all out in his belief and practice of his own faith, not in spite of such commitment.[12]

The Catholic theologian, Professor Karl Adam, explained that

> since Buchman is not aiming to build another Christian church, but to re-create personal experience of the moral and religious *a priori* from which all living religions begin, it is understandable that numerous non-Christians from India, China, Japan and so on are among the convinced followers of the movement.[13]

Increasingly people of goodwill from different faiths and creeds have been coming together in the common fight against materialism – against evil in all its forms. They have been taking their stand on those moral and spiritual essentials at the heart of the great religions, not on dogmas which divide but on the truths which unite. It was in this spirit that Pope John Paul II took the initiative for the unprecedented gathering of a hundred representatives of

27

various faiths at Assisi in 1986.

Cardinal Franz König of Vienna called Buchman 'a turning-point in the modern world ... The fundamental struggle', he said, 'is not so much between systems as in the daily choices in human hearts and wills of people ... His great idea was to show that the teaching of Jesus Christ is not just a private affair but has the great force to change the whole structure of the social orders of economics, of political ideas, if we combine the changing of structures with a change of heart.'[14]

Although 'revolution' in Buchman's sense is spiritual and non-violent, it is more exacting than ordinary revolution because it means giving everything.

> There were some people in the Acts and the Gospels who gave everything. There were others who did not give everything. Even in a revolution some people want an amount of padding around them. I want to ask you this morning whether you want to be that kind of revolutionary. If so, there may be a comfortable place for you behind the lines. But somewhere on the battlefront we will have the real revolutionaries.[15]

The vision which is part of spiritual revolution leads to personal rebirth or renaissance, as the starting point of renaissance on a world scale.

> We haven't begun to experience the spiritual revolution we need. You need revolution, and then when you come into the clear light of God's presence you will experience a glorious renaissance.[16]

Because it is a spiritual revolution of rebirth, it does not destroy the old order any more than it destroys people; instead, it builds on the best in the old order and regenerates it, just as it builds on the best in people and so changes them. It is a revolution which can 'save and recreate a society on the brink of collapse.'[17]

To take part in this revolution demands a definite decision. 'In an age of material revolution [those so deciding] have enlisted in a spiritual revolution.' This does not merely lead to participation in a revolution: *it brings the revolution about.* At the same time, enlistment is 'only an initial experience. Enlistment does not immediately make the trained soldier, but we can all begin.'[18]

This is the beginning of the 'full dimension of change, economic change, social change, national change, international change – all based on personal change.'[19] As a spiritual revolution it transforms both personal life and the life of society at one and the same time; change in the person and change in 'the system' take place together. 'Human nature changes and human society changes.'[20]

We must build on the gains in political and economic structures through the upsurges of the past few hundred years. Hans Boeckler, Chairman of the Trade Unions in the British Zone of Germany and an architect of West Germany's postwar 'economic miracle', said after meeting Buchman and his friends in 1949, 'when men change, the structure of society changes, and when the structure of society changes, men change. Both go together and both are necessary.' This parallels Jean Monnet's belief that when people change in the way they act, these changes must be incorporated in rules and institutions if they are to last. 'Experience begins over again with every man. Institutions alone become wiser: they accumulate the general experience,' he said, quoting the Swiss philosopher Henri-Frédéric Amiel. Although sceptical of changes in human nature, he believed that good structures lead to good behaviour. With these convictions he initiated the construction of the first European Community.[21] The structures of the United Nations are also a positive outcome of the two World Wars, adapting in recent years to enlarged responsibilities in peace-making and peace-keeping, with an array of institutions for health, education and humanitarian relief.

Despite such achievements the future of the world is still in doubt. But if comparisons with Antiquity are valid, we can take comfort from the fact that it took all the five centuries of the Hellenistic period for the mind-change with its philosophic and religious accompaniments to come to fruition, and an even longer period for new civilisations to be created – altogether some seven centuries. We can reckon that the West's modern 'Hellenistic Age', beginning with the spiritual upsurge of Renaissance and Reformation, has continued with varying degrees of intensity for nearly six centuries already. It may well be that we are coming into the last phase of this upsurge, bringing changes comparable to those which led on to the coming of the new civilisations at the end of Antiquity.

Frank Buchman's work can best be seen in this perspective. It is in the tradition of those men and women, while the power of that vast spiritual upsurge was gathering, whose concern was for personal change and seeking the 'inner light' of God's guidance, with meetings for prayer, Bible-study and mutual encouragement.

30

It meant applying Christ's words 'the kingdom of God is within you'[22] – the believer should be 'so walking on earth, that he doth in a sort carry his heaven with him.' The 'divine seed', the indwelling Spirit, could perfect a man's nature – this was the real change, all else, including the form in which those called of God should meet or worship together, being secondary.

It is the beginning of a quiet and on-going revolution which can often appear as affecting only the lives of individuals and families, but which in fact has formed the main stream of dedicated Christian living in Western Europe, or rather in 'the West' as a whole. This stream early divided, running in various regions, sometimes underground, but welling up to provide the dynamism and mystique for effective action at crucial moments in society and politics. In recent times the confluence of three major streams, in Continental Protestantism, Roman Catholic radicalism, and Anglo-American endeavour made possible the first real act of statesmanship in Europe since the end of the second World War, the creation of the European Community.[23]

In its early years in England and Scotland this stream continued to flow despite the persecution of such as George Fox and John Bunyan under the restored monarchy, with a renewed upsurge in the 18th century through John and Charles Wesley, which was carried on into the 19th by William Wilberforce and many others.

From a fresh source in the University of Halle (Saxony), this stream in the mid-18th century flowed into America. One of the greatest bearers of this new life was Henry Muhlenberg, sent out at

31

the request of German-speaking colonists.[24] This tradition remained strong in America during the 19th century, constantly renewed by Dwight Moody and others. Important in this connection were universities on both sides of the Atlantic, a development in which Henry Drummond played a large part.

It was maintaining its power in the early 20th century, as witness the response which John R. Mott found during his visits to Oxford and Cambridge in 1908. At Oxford almost the entire student body of 3,000 attended his meetings, with three lectures for dons, a meeting for women, and at the conclusion a closed gathering of 230 men 'selected from the 21 colleges with reference to their powers of leadership.' The Muslim students were not neglected – he had breakfast with them, while the rowing men and other sportsmen gave him lunch at Vincent's. During this visit a 'large number' of undergraduates requested interviews.[25]

The Christian spirituality of the 19th century on both sides of the Atlantic had the effect of bringing reformers like Shaftesbury to initiate improvements in working and social conditions for the mass of the population, and began to influence policy in international affairs. In France as the Crimean War was threatening, Alphonse Gratry appealed for a Christian nation to set its course 'for peace and not war as the honour and glory of peoples,' and so give a lead in breaking the tradition of warfare as a means of settling disputes.[26] This preceded by nearly a century Frank Buchman's call for Switzerland to be 'a prophet among the nations and a peacemaker in the international family'.[27] Gratry was in the tradition of French radical Catholicism, pioneered in the 19th century by Lammenais and Lacordaire, which continued at the Collège St. Stanislas after his directorship there. At the end of the century, as a student at St. Stanislas, Marc Sangnier initiated the Sillon movement which helped to mould the Christian statesmanship of Robert Schuman, the architect of the European Community.[28]

The Gratry Society was founded, and reconstituted in 1906, backed by Sangnier and his 'Sillon' friends: its aim was an 'active commitment to putting Christian principles to work in politics', and especially to proclaim that 'the principles of Christian morality apply as much to relations among peoples as the relations among individuals.'

1914 had seen the eclipse of all such efforts. Sangnier himself served with distinction at the front. After the war most of his energy went into striving for a peace settlement both just and fair, while working for reconciliation with Germany. He anticipated the European Community in calling for an economic agreement between France and Germany as the first step towards integrating both countries in an international 'entente' – but the time for creating the necessary structures had not arrived. It was still a question of creating heart or 'soul', *'un nouvel état d'âme international'*, and in striving to do this Sangnier was indefatigable.

As a member of the *'horizon bleu'* Parliament immediately after the 1914-18 war, he took an independent line, often as a lone voice. There and in public gatherings he castigated the self-contradictory policy of suppressing Germany while exacting huge sums in reparations, instead of promoting the construction of a peaceful Europe. He organised vast demonstrations, starting with an international peace congress at Paris in December 1921, the first such occasion to which Germans were invited after the war. Another was held in Germany, at the moment when France was occupying the Ruhr in order to force reparations payment – a policy strongly contested by Sangnier in Parliament. Occasions which he arranged on his estate at Bierville, designed particularly to attract young people, were more than just demonstrations. In 1926 six thousand came for a month of meetings, courses, music and plays (an open-air theatre was built). Three aircraft hangers end-to-end held twenty thousand for special meetings, at which, among other things, racism and colonialism were condemned. But Europe had to tear itself in pieces once more before a way could be found to direct such enthusiasm into the creation of new structures for ensuring peace.

Sangnier's brand of radicalism eventually found its political expression in the Parti démocrate populaire (PDP) formed by some of his followers in 1924. Its platform was explicitly Christian, envisaging an improvement in the conditions of the underprivileged and workers, and ensuring the latter a fair share in the running of industry; and a foreign policy 'resolutely French' while 'definitely favourable to the methods of international collaboration'. This was the party which in 1931 Robert Schuman joined, to earn himself in the post-war years the title of 'Father of Europe' for his part in founding the European Community. Sangnier held himself aloof from the PDP (he was no longer in Parliament during those years) concentrating his efforts at his Bierville centre on 'education in depth, the transformation of individuals', and so sending forth 'currents' which later led to the creation by others of new structures in society and politics.

Some of his followers, after using the old 'Sillon' premises as a Resistance base during the German occupation, changed their group, 'Les nouvelles équipes françaises', into a political party, the Mouvement républicain populaire (MRP) with Sangnier as Honorary President. The party was successful at the polls in October 1945, attracting nearly a third of the electorate. Schuman was one of those elected on the MRP ticket.[29]

Meanwhile an initiative on the German side prepared the way for reconciliation between France and Germany. The Nazis had killed most of the leading Christian dissidents, among them Dietrich Bonhoeffer and Helmuth von Moltke, with their visions of a united Europe, but Martin Niemöller survived. The Declaration of Guilt, made by him, Bishop Wurm and Karl Barth, at a conference at Stuttgart in November 1945, and the enlightened policy of French officials in their occupation zone, led up to the meetings of French and Germans at the Caux conferences of 1946 and following years.[30]

References

1. A. Chouraqui: *Ce que je crois* (Paris 1979), 256, 308, 160

2. Interview in *Le Monde*, 13/4/93

3. *Ce que je crois* (Paris 1979), 146, 336; *Lettre à un ami chrétien* (Paris 1971), 199; *Retour aux racines* (Paris 1981), 254

4. 147, New York, 23/4/46

5. Dr Charis Waddy (letter to author). The quotations are from FB: 147, New York, 23/4/46 and 41, London, 9/8/36

6. Mark, 12: 29-31

7. 22/3/93

8. M.K. Gandhi: *The Message of Jesus Christ* (Bharatiya Vidya Bhavan, Bombay 1964), 36, 38

9. FB: 167, California, June 1948

10. FB: 215, Morocco, December 1953

11. FB: 231, London, 4/6/56

12. Dr Charis Waddy (letter to author)

13. Cited FB: 374

14. Garth Lean: *Frank Buchman – a Life* (London 1985), 2, 532

15. FB: 56, Visby, 16/8/38

16. FB: 148, New York, 23/4/46

17. FB: 161, Caux, 15/7/47

18. FB: 58, Visby

19. FB: 171, Caux, 4/6/49

20. FB: 187, Gelsenkirchen, 4/6/50

21. R.C. Mowat: *Creating the European Community* (London 1973), 60

22. F.E. Stoeffler: *The Rise of Evangelical Pietism* (Leiden 1965), 85 (citing from Joseph Hall)

23. RCM, 108-9

24. RCM, 110

25. John R. Mott: *Addresses and Papers* (New York 1947) II, 356-7; RCM 148

26. Alphonse Gratry: *Philosophie de la connaissance de l'âme* (Paris 1857), II, 491; RCM 145

27. FB: 18, Zurich, 6/10/35

28. RCM, 149ff

29. RCM, 191-2

30. See Ch. 6, pp. 47ff; RCM, 194-5

CHAPTER 5

THE CREATIVE MINORITY

If we are at the beginning of another upsurge, the tiniest inputs may determine how it develops. Almost infinitesimal changes in certain initial conditions can have enormous effects on the outcome; or, as the French mathematician Henri Poincaré put it, 'small differences in the initial conditions produce great ones in the final phenomena.'[1] A colourful simile is presented in meteorological terms by E. Lorenz: 'The flap of a butterfly's wings in Brazil' could 'set off a tornado in Texas.' The 19th century Scottish physicist James Clerk Maxwell made the same point in scientific terms: 'Immeasurably small differences in input can produce entirely different outcomes for the system.'[2]

Brian Keenan, the Beirut hostage, said: 'I know now that I make history in every touch I have with people, even how I greet people in the street.' H.W. Brands points out that 'individuals, faced with specific decisions, are unpredictable [but] people in groups, acting over time, tend to be less so ... Patterns emerge and predictability becomes possible.'[3]

Buchman saw such groups fusing to make 'a force in action with the answer, available for service',[4] or, as a 'spearhead, an arrow, pointing to the solution for a world in chaos.'[5]... They will be an incomparable, unconquerable, irresistible army,' with 'the strategy to win the world from her egocentric ways.'[6]

Each new type of society has been the work of what A.J. Toynbee calls a 'creative minority'.[7] This may be regarded as a 'cell' or nucleus, composed of people who are changing society – are themselves a microcosm or embryo of the new society. From one aspect it is a growing point of the new world order; from another it is the instrument under God for bringing it in. 'There is a tremendous power in a minority guided by God,' said Buchman.[8] 'That power active in a minority can be the solvent of a whole country's problems.'[9]

So with the world as a whole. The renewal or remaking of civilisation 'depends on and awaits the emergence in every country of firm and resolute God-guided men, with all the conviction, fire and fervour of early Christians. Their ever-widening influence would be invincible ... if in every country there would arise a new leadership, free from the bondage of fear, rising above personal and national ambition and responsive to the direction of God's will.'[10] In seeing 'this divinely appointed destiny of mankind' in terms of the Christians whose leavening influence saved the best remnants of the decaying Greco-Roman civilisation, Buchman was showing a sound historical sense. In that period, the early centuries AD, the Christians undoubtedly were in the van of those who were bringing new life in manners and morals, in politics, finance and administration, in all aspects of culture, in place of outmoded and decadent forms.

The basis of their action was moral change, the teaching of the Sermon on the Mount. The 'splendid and stringent moral code'

39

which each candidate for baptism had to accept, when 'every sin was tracked to its lurking-place within', went far beyond the challenge of its rivals, and for this reason had for many the greatest possible attraction. Although the work of the apostles and travelling teachers was an essential part of spreading the Gospel, it was the way of life as lived by most ordinary Christians during the early period of the Church which was impressive. 'For over a century and a half it ranked everything almost secondary to the supreme task of maintaining its morality' – its mission 'might be described as a moral enterprise, as the awakening and strengthening of the moral sense.' It demonstrated on a hitherto undreamed of scale the way in which men and women could care for each other, in maintaining their commitment and fulfilling their duties, with a thorough-going service of help for the sick and for those otherwise in need. The fact that Christians also included pagans in their relief work during times of famine or plague further enhanced their appeal.[11]

In setting their sights on a realm under God's rule beyond this life, and combating the evil as they saw it in this world, the early Christians (along with Stoics and many of the other faiths impelled by the spiritual upsurge of the time) created two new civilisations, Byzantium and the Latin West, with a strong influence on that of Islam.

The creative minority of that period did not know that they were rebuilding civilisation – they thought the world was doomed and its destruction was at hand. This shows that the renewing process is only partly due to the conscious actions of people. It is the parable of the sower and the seed. The farmer has to sow the seed, but then it grows 'he knows not how' – and if it is sown on good ground it will bring forth fruit 'an hundredfold'.[12]

It can also be compared to that of leaven in the dough, which works by the rapid multiplication of cells in order to produce bread, or to any other organism, for instance a plant or tree, which grows while maintaining its own essential nature until it overshadows the entire area around. From small beginnings it grows like the 'seed' mentioned in St Mark's Gospel[13] until it becomes 'greater than all herbs,' shooting out 'great branches, so that the fowls of the air may lodge under the shadow of it.' In other words, the organism of the new society grows until it is big enough to overshadow or embrace in some measure the entire world.

The process is spontaneous, different from joining a club or any other organisation. Said Buchman: 'It is a quality of life. You don't join and you can't resign. You live a life.'[14] This is the 'world organism that takes the needs of nations and answers them with men ... It unites all in the world-organism of God-directed men and women, the responsible family of mankind.'[15]

An organism – the metaphor of biological cells is relevant.

Such cells are formed spontaneously as soon as a person finds the experience of change and begins to pass it on. 'When I changed, I found the spirit of those around me changed. We learnt to pull together. We learnt to unite.'[16]

On the quality of life of the home depends its effectiveness as a cell.

Ask yourself how many really happy homes you know – and the home is the basis of the nation's life. Ask yourself, 'Is your home governed by a democracy or a dictatorship?' I fear that many, all too many, ardent advocates of democracy reserve for themselves the right to be dictators in their own home. Selfish in the home, they have no constructive programme for a selfish world.

Disunity in the home makes disunity in the nation. Compromise and conflict sap the power of national life. Countless families everywhere, who want peace in the world, are waging a private war of their own, and so are robbing their country of a united effort. Thus democracy, too, misses in practice the experience of a God-led nation.

Homes with this force in everyday life will secure the next generation from chaos.[17]

References

1. *Diplomatic History*, 16 (Fall 1992), H.W. Brands: 'Fractal History, or Clio and the Chaotics', 497-8

2. *International History*, vol. 17, 3 (1992/3): John L. Gaddis: 'Danger in paradigms'

3. Brands, ibid., 503

4. FB: 158, Caux, 15/7/47

5. FB: 13, Oxford, 28/7/35

6. FB: 114, 112, USA, 29/10/39

7. A.J. Toynbee: *A Study of History* (Oxford 1934), IV, 5,6

8. FB: 63, Interlaken, 6/9/38

9. FB: 46, East Ham, 29/5/38

10. FB: 111, USA, 29/10/39

11. A. Harnack: *The Expansion of Christianity in the first three Centuries* (London 1904), I, 487-8, 258; quoted in RCM 45

12. Mark 4: 27,20

13. Mark 4: 31-2

14. FB: 114, USA, 29/10/39

15. FB: 66, 67, Interlaken, 10/9/38

16. FB: 83, London, November 1938

17. FB: 79, London, 27/11/38: 161, Caux, 15/7/47

CHAPTER 6

INTERNATIONAL RELATIONS

Carl Hambro, besides presiding over the Norwegian Parliament, chaired the Supervisory Council of the League of Nations. Addressing a meeting of British Members of Parliament at the House of Commons in December 1933, he characterised the crisis at that time as a chronic period of degeneration, where civilisation is killed by its own products.

> The atmosphere [was] of futility and ineffectiveness at the League in Geneva – the feeling that the fundamental questions have never been touched, that only the minor and secondary problems have been tackled ... the insincerity with which debates are usually carried on there, with no sense of the vital issues at stake ... The continual deadlocks in politics are in fact because we have not accepted in international relations the honesty which we demand, or which rather Christianity demands in ordinary life. Absolute honesty in politics would go a long way towards putting right the world's political problems – especially when allied with absolute charity. And there England had very much of the blame to bear, with her previous attitude of 'my country right or wrong'; for the principle of absolute love meant no less than considering *other* countries as well as one's own ... He could see the possibility – he had a vision of all the delegates before a conference sharing together their views and plans in a spirit of absolute honesty and love – and if they did so, how completely different these conferences would be.[1]

A few years later Frank Buchman developed this thought:

> Any of us can recall a succession of conferences which started with high hopes but ended with failure. Yet conferences, God-controlled, would surprise everyone, because they would be successful and accomplish what they set out to do.[2]

These words and those of Hambro, which may have seemed visionary at the time, came near to fulfilment a few years later. With the defeat of Hitler and Mussolini and their abettors in France, remarkable statesmen appeared in their place, Adenauer, De Gasperi and Schuman, devoted Catholics who were committed to building peace. Monnet, Spaak and others, while not claiming 'God-control' as their principle, nonetheless brought a spirit of mutual understanding, openness and honesty. Schuman in particular gave a sense of God-inspired direction to their deliberations. Hence the speed with which their governments accepted Schuman's Declaration of 9 May 1950, launching the first European Community, and the success of the Conference of Paris the next year, where the necessary details were agreed.[3]

By their action these statesmen transformed France and Germany from being hereditary enemies into partners. 'Divine guidance is the only practical politics', Buchman said,[4] and Schuman was pre-eminent among European statesmen in applying this principle. He cast aside the old 'weapons of statesmanship' which, in Buchman's words, 'seem like relics from the armoury of some illustrious ancestor, which in their day were useful, but now, outmoded, leave us defeated and defenceless'[5] ... When at home at Scy-Chazelles near Metz, Schuman would seek God's guidance daily at early Mass in the little chapel opposite his house. In following his inspired hunches, he balanced boldness with caution. André Philip, one of his former Cabinet colleagues and close collaborator, described his approach:

> Often he has tacked about, delayed the decision, tried to dodge the call which was making itself felt in the depths of his conscience; then, when there was nothing more to do, when he was sure of what the inner voice was demanding, he took the boldest initiative and pushed it to its conclusion, equally heedless of attacks as of threats.[6]

His ultimate concern was with building Christian civilisation.

> Christ's kingdom was not of this world. That means also that Christian civilisation should not be the product of a violent and sudden revolution, but of a progressive transformation, of a patient education, under the action of the great principles of caring, of sacrifice and of humility, which are the foundations of the new society.[7]

This 'patient education' concerned Schuman as much as his parliamentary work. He saw it as part of a 'vast programme of expanding democracy ... which finds its flowering in the making of Europe'.[8]

His concern for the 'patient education' of the public is apparent from his early years. As a young man in German-occupied Metz he joined the Union Populaire Catholique Lorraine, which looked to the spiritual unity of Alsace-Lorraine with France, Belgium and Luxembourg. He kept the press-cutting of a meeting in 1913 when the leading speaker said 'Vous êtes une école d'apostolat par votre influence et votre vie.' Schuman spoke next with a call to study the needs of the workers and to become well-informed about social and political affairs: 'Let us be clear about our mission as apostles.'[9] Years later the same thoughts reappear in his foreword to the French edition of Frank Buchman's *Remaking the World*.[10]

First the call to mutual education:

> What we need, and what is quite new, is a school where, by a process of mutual teaching, we can work out our practical behaviour towards each other; a school where Christian principles are not only applied and proven in the relationships of man to man, but succeed in overcoming the prejudices and enmities which separate classes, races and nations. To begin by creating a moral climate in which true brotherly unity can flourish, over-arching all that today tears the world apart – that is the immediate goal.

Then the practical method, the 'apostolate'.

> The acquisition of wisdom about men and their affairs by bringing people together in public assemblies and personal encounters – that is the means employed. To provide teams of trained men, ready for the service of the state, apostles of reconciliation and builders of a new world, that is the beginning of a far-reaching transformation of society in which, during fifteen war-ravaged years, the first steps have already been taken. It is not a question of a change of policy; it is a question of changing men. Democracy and her freedoms can be saved only by the quality of the men who speak in her name.

Schuman was referring to the conferences at Caux, the centre established in 1946 by Swiss adherents of Moral Re-Armament (MRA). He had realised, before taking over as Foreign Minister of France in 1948, how much change had to take place in the hearts

47

and minds of his fellow-citizens before a policy of reconciliation with Germany could bring to fruition the initiatives of Niemöller and others. Trade unionists would not attend international conferences at which Germans (though anti-Nazis) were present. He had to wait until enough of the public were ready for such a move. At this preparatory stage – and later – the Caux conferences made a significant contribution.

In its village setting in the mountains above the Lake of Geneva, Caux proved a magnet for many of Europe's postwar leaders from all walks of life. With permits obtained from the occupation authorities in the western zones, several thousand Germans came in the immediate postwar years, among them Konrad Adenauer, the future Chancellor of the Federal Republic, and the Ministers-President of the newly established Länder (states), along with industrialists and trade union leaders. The change in some of the French whom they met made a particularly powerful impression. One of these was Mme Irène Laure, who had been a Resistance leader and Socialist M.P. for Marseilles. Disillusioned after efforts in the interwar years to build bridges between French and Germans, her hatred of the Germans became intense during the occupation. She came to Caux expecting it to be a capitalist trap – her suspicion turned to repulsion when she found there were Germans present. She was on the point of leaving when a talk with Buchman left her with the uncomfortable thought, 'can you build the new Europe without the Germans?' After three days and nights of agonized ponderings, she stood up in full conference with the words: 'I hated Germany so much that I would have liked to see it erased from the map of Europe. But I have seen here that my hatred is wrong. I would like to ask the Germans present to forgive me.'

The effect on the Germans was electric. One of them related that he could not sleep for several nights – his 'whole past was in revolt at the courage of this woman'. The full horror of the things their country had done came over them. They decided to apologise to Mme. Laure, and publicly admit their shame, while undertaking to work in the spirit which she had shown, to rebuild Europe on new foundations.

Soon after, Mme. Laure was invited to Germany, where she addressed two hundred meetings in eleven weeks, making several subsequent visits, eight of them to Berlin, including the time it was blockaded by the Russians. She spoke to many thousands in the Western zones, addressing the representatives of the Länder parliaments, and meeting the men and women who were coming forward into public life. Others from France went with her, among them two men who had lost most of their families, the one fifteen and the other twenty-two, in the gas-chambers. Such actions played their part in preparing the ground for the political decisions which made it possible for the statesmen to carry through on another level the work of reconciliation and open a new way towards the future of Western Europe.[11]

Though Schuman was responsible for launching the Plan and ensuring its approval by the Cabinet and Parliament as well as by the steel-masters, the Community of Coal and Steel could never have been created without the co-operation of other statesmen who were formed in the Christian tradition: Adenauer and De Gasperi, Jean Monnet, and the Belgian leader Paul Henri Spaak – men who were capable together of seizing the moment which could change the course of history. Nor could it have proved acceptable to Parliament and the other interests concerned in France – perhaps not in Germany either – without a revolution in public opinion in both countries which prepared the way for replacing inherited hatreds with partnership. Here again the spiritual factor played a part, through the humility, vision and tireless self-giving of a few dedicated fellow-citizens. It was a convergence of spiritual currents: the Christian-based humanism and pragmatism of the Zonal officials and Jean Monnet; the Lutheran-Pietist tradition of Bonhoeffer and Niemöller; the Roman Catholic inheritance of Adenauer and De Gasperi, and its radical tradition coming down to Schuman from Lamennais, Gratry and Sangnier, combining with the Anglo-American stream descending through Moody, Drummond, Mott and Buchman.

These were the creative springs of the greatest act of statesmanship in 20th century Europe. Stalin's rapacity, the Communist menace and American pressure – all played their part in bringing the politicians to their decisions and the public to their support, but without the spiritual factor operating through men and women of character and commitment, their work could hardly have been well-based, with the organism that was its outcome so well adapted for further evolution. The novel economic and political structure which the statesmen initiated, to become eventually the European Community, and within which the age-old enmity of France and Germany was replaced by reconciliation and friendship, may mark the beginning of a new order rather than merely revitalising the old.[12]

References

1. Letter from author to R.B. and M.G. Mowat (9/12/33), quoted in RCM: 307

2. FB: 68, Geneva, 15/9/38

3. RCM: *Creating the European Community*, 118-9

4. FB: 18, Zurich, 6/10/35

5. FB: 100, California, 22/7/39

6. *France-Forum*, November 1963

7. Robert Schuman: *Pour l'Europe* (Paris 1963), 66

8. Ibid., 77

9. R. Rochefort: *Robert Schuman* (Paris 1968), 55, 57

10. *Refaire le monde* (Paris 1950); FB: 347

11. RCM: 196-7

12. RCM: 207-8, 298-9; Douglas Johnson, Hal Saunders & associates: *The missing dimension of statecraft* (Grosvenor Books, London 1993, and the Center for Strategic and International Studies, Washington DC, USA). Their book *Religion: the Missing Dimension of Statecraft* is to be published by the Oxford University Press in 1994.

CHAPTER 7

POLITICS

'It is possible,' said Buchman, 'for the Mind of God to become the mind of nations.'[1] In such cases leadership would go 'to the spiritually fit,' for the people would 'naturally choose as leaders those who are most clearly led by God.'[2] He was fond of quoting William Penn: 'Men must choose to be governed by God or they condemn themselves to be ruled by tyrants.'[3]

An example from the 15th century of such a statesman is St Nikolaus von der Flüe,

> who had this gift of divine direction. As he exercised it, he became the saviour of his country. He was a farmer who tilled his land well, a soldier, a magistrate. At fifty, oppressed by the problems of a warring world, he gave up much to follow radically the guidance of God. Soon his inspired good sense, knowledge of men and singleness of heart commanded the respect of his contemporaries, not only in Switzerland but in all Europe. He became the most sought-after arbiter in affairs of state. When the bitter quarrels of the Cantons brought his country to the verge of civil war it was his God-given answer which set Switzerland on the good road that gave her unity.[4]

For Buchman it was a progression: 'A new type of man, a new type of statesmanship, a new type of national policy[5] ... Government, as one Prime Minister said, is then made easier. For the more men, under God, govern themselves, the less they need government from outside.'[6]

Abraham Lincoln and Frank Buchman both spoke to America and the world with the voice of prophets. In his speeches Buchman refers to Lincoln and quotes him several times – he was evidently one of those in the previous centuries who inspired him most.

Lincoln's overriding concern was saving the United States of America – saving the Union by preventing the secession of the Southern states where slavery was permitted. He believed this was necessary, even at the cost of civil war, not only for America but for the world. God's plan, he believed, was to show in the USA that a country of continental dimensions could be a true democracy. 'We shall nobly save, or meanly lose, the last, best hope on earth.' (Message to Congress, 1/12/1862). The Union was saved, slavery was officially abolished, but real integration remained a dream – integration between South and North, between former slaves or their descendants and those that were free. To move towards complete integration it needed Martin Luther King's 'dream' and the work of people like Frank Buchman, who inspired the musical play (later filmed) *The Crowning Experience*. With the black singer, Muriel Smith, in the lead part, this was put on at the crisis of the integration struggle at Atlanta in 1958, and led to the change of attitude by the formerly anti-integrationist Governor of Arkansas, Orval Faubus, and his reconciliation with Mrs L.C. Bates, a leader of the National Association for the Advancement of Colored People.[7]

Buchman played a major part in consolidating the work of Lincoln in America. But well before the handshake of Mrs Bates and Faubus at Little Rock, the basis of civilisation in America and

Europe was being undermined by moral decline. Where Lincoln's main concern was the survival of a united America, essential to the fulfilment (he believed) of God's plan in the world, Buchman's main concern was the saving of civilisation there and elsewhere. He did not neglect America – in 1940 he called for 'the moral and spiritual defence of the nation' and focused on creating industrial co-operation and national unity as war-time priorities. But already in Europe and America he had raised the issue: 'Is it to be God's light of a new day for Europe and the world; or is it to be the fading light of a doomed civilisation?[8] ... Until we deal with human nature thoroughly and drastically on a national scale, nations must still follow their historic road to violence and destruction.'[9]

Buchman recalls Lincoln's experience of God's guidance – how he 'listened [to God] at a time of crisis and preserved a nation's unity.'[10] Lincoln spoke about God's 'plan of dealing with this nation ... I think He means that we shall do more than we have yet done in furtherance of His plans, and He will open the way for our doing it. I have felt His hand upon me and have submitted to His guidance, and I trust that as He shall further open the way I will be ready to walk therein relying on His help and trusting in His goodness and wisdom.'[11]

Lincoln also believed that God's purposes for a *nation* could be perceived. In his Proclamation of 7 July 1864 for a Day of Prayer, Lincoln asked his fellow-citizens to pray earnestly that God would 'enlighten the mind of the Nation to know and do His will that our place should be maintained as a united people among the family of nations.'[12]

God speaking to the nation. That was Frank Buchman's concept too. In his vision it could happen in any country where a fully committed minority would listen to God. Lincoln was dependent on the support of such a minority in his day, like the group represented by Mrs Eliza Gurney and three other Quaker Friends, whom he received at a deeply moving occasion at the White House.[13]

'God's purposes are perfect and must prevail,' said Lincoln. According to his biographer, 'the idea that there could be direct communication between finite minds and the definite [?infinite] Mind became for Lincoln an idea of overwhelming magnitude ... His chief form of prayer was seeking to know what the will of God really is' – though he was well aware of human fallibility: 'the purposes of God must prevail, though we erring mortals may fail accurately to perceive them in advance.'[14]

In this context one of Lincoln's statements (part of which is quoted in *Remaking the World*) is particularly relevant.[15]

> That the Almighty does make use of human agencies, and directly intervenes in human affairs, is one of the plainest statements of the Bible. I have had so many evidences of His direction, so many instances when I have been controlled by some other power than my own will, that I cannot doubt that this power comes from above. I frequently see my way clear to a decision when I have no sufficient facts upon which to found it. I am satisfied that when the Almighty wants me to do or not to do a particular thing, He finds a way of letting me know it. I am confident that it is His design to restore the Union. He will do it in His own good time.[16]

When the Civil War was coming to its end, Lincoln referred in his Second Inaugural to American slavery as one of those offences which God 'wills to remove, and that he gives to both North and South this terrible war, as the woe due to those by whom the offence came.'[17]

Wars, famines, epidemics and other horrors of various kinds may be 'woes' or divine judgements. As in Antiquity, things may go on for some time getting worse before they begin to get better – assuming that progress takes place before the habitat is irreversibly wrecked. But when a better era dawns, our contribution will not be quantifiable. It will be because God is at work, bringing about 'one of those great transactions in history which men will often not regard when they are passing before them, but which they look back upon with awe and astonishment some years after they are past.'[18]

References

1. FB: 113, USA, 29/10/39

2. FB: 66, Interlaken, 10/9/38

3. FB: 241, Mackinac, June 1957

4. FB: 154, Caux, 4/6/47

5. FB: 187, Gelsenkirchen, 4/6/50

6. FB: 66, Interlaken, 10/9/38

7. FB: 266-7, Caux, 4/6/60. Lean: 499ff

8. FB: 65, Interlaken, 10/9/38

9. FB: 38, Birmingham, 26/7/36

10. FB: 121, USA, 2/12/39

11. E. Trueblood: *Abraham Lincoln* (New York 1973), 126-7

12. Trueblood, 93

13. Trueblood, 42ff

14. Trueblood, 90, 77, 123, 45

15. FB: 131, USA, 4/6/40

16. Trueblood, 128

17. Trueblood, 124

18. Trueblood, 120, citing John Bright

CHAPTER 8

STAGES IN WORLD CHANGE

After the first civilisations formed it took many centuries for the new type of society to spread throughout the world. In comparison with those days, history is now moving at breakneck speed. Even so the process of change to a new type of society must be expected to take generations rather than a few decades. There will be a considerable time-gap between the new way of life as lived by people in a limited number of groups or centres, and by people on the world scale.

Change takes place first as a change of tone or direction. In a home, one changed person can change its whole tone, even before the other members of the family have consciously accepted change; so in a business, factory, trade union, office, school.

In Streeter's words:

> History shows that in case of wars, revolutions, strikes and other major conflicts, a relatively small weight of public opinion on the one side or the other, or the presence or absence of moral insight and courage in a few individuals in positions of influence, has often turned the balance between a reasonable settlement and a fight to the finish. Modern civilisation can only be saved by a moral revival. But for this it would suffice if every tenth or hundredth person were changed. For each such person raises the level of those whom he touches in the home, in business, and in public affairs.[1]

Schweitzer says:

> The beginning of all spiritual life of any real value is courageous faith in truth and open confession of the same.[2]

As Buchman sees it:

> In a day when selfishness and expediency are the common practice of men and nations... people have written off the four standards [absolute honesty, purity, unselfishness and love] as part of the horse-and-buggy days. So, naturally, they are the last thing they have in mind for nations. That is why you have the condition there is in the world today. Now if you can get people who will live up to these absolutes and stand for them, then you have a force, a creative something in the community with a strength that nothing will gainsay.[3]

So in a nation and eventually in the world as a whole. The first stage is the creation of a new 'mental climate' within nations – even one nation taking a lead in this way will create a new mental climate in the world.[4]

> If this miracle is to come into the world some nation must give a lead. Some nation must find God's will as her destiny and God-guided men as her representatives at home and abroad.[5]

The final stage is the acceptance 'by everyone everywhere' of the new ideas and their accompanying way of life.[6]

*   *   *   *   *   *

As we look back to the 1930's we can understand the urgency of Buchman and many others from every background so to bring about changes that the war, which was threatening, might be averted –

Buchman speaks of 'a race with time to remake men and nations.'[7] The point was, and is, that while God's purposes may work out over centuries, anyone who receives a call from Him should obey NOW. The great question for us is, can we help to speed up these changes before catastrophe intervenes, or before the destruction of the habitat is irreversible?

'Are we beginning to see,' Frank Buchman asked in 1935, 'that not only individuals but cities and nations may be different?'[8] He cited Norway where, according to Carl Hambro, 'hundreds and thousands of lives have been changed' with the consequence (said the national newspaper *Tidens Tegn*) that 'the mental outlook of the country has definitely changed.' Hambro added (referring to Buchman and his team) that 'the Oxford Group has also conquered Denmark in a way that none of us would have thought possible.'[9]

Streeter was one of those who helped to bring about this change. As he wrote later:

> I went with the Group to Denmark three times, and what I saw there convinced me that the movement was not merely an instrument of moral rebirth and psychological liberation for individuals, but was capable of moving nations as such by initiating a new mental attitude in economic and political conflicts.
>
> Evidence accumulated of the effect on the conduct of everyday life. We heard, for example, of a rise in the standard of commercial honesty in certain circles in the capital, of a readiness in leading politicians to approach the discussion of burning economic problems in a spirit of friendly and constructive conference rather than in one of party bitterness

and intrigue. Customs officers reported an unfamiliar influx of conscience money, and there has been a marked diminution in the statistics of divorce. Thus in one country, in the space of one year, there has been born a new spirit in facing the conflicts which threatened the collapse of civilisation.[10]

In his sermon in the English church in Copenhagen on Palm Sunday 1935 Streeter said:

The prejudices of one set of people, the financial interests of another, too great deference by national leaders to public opinion in one way or another, and similar influences, have brought about a situation in which the conflict of race and class, prejudices and interests, has become so acute that the slightest error in the juggling of the diplomatic balls may precipitate a world war. Respite is no cure if, when the thing comes, it will be worse than if it had not been postponed. But there is one chance. Can we somehow or other make use of such a respite – and it may be quite a short one – to do something which is going to bring about in Europe a fundamental moral change? During the war everyone was anxious to do his bit. Today to do your bit for the salvation of civilisation means to begin with the reform of yourself ... To pocket your pride and give yourself away may be the great cross which you personally ought to face this week. For you, facing that cross may be the necessary path to a spiritual resurrection.[11]

Denmark was a small country, but the challenge was clear. If one country could change enough to give a lead, a new future could open for Europe and the world. But before the respite of which Streeter spoke had ended in the disaster of World War II, he himself, with his wife Irene, had met his end in a plane crash in 1937.

Norway and Denmark maintained this spirit throughout the war, before and during the German occupation. In Denmark, according to one account:

> We decided that we needed to move from personal change in the direction of national change. The new spirit which had permeated the group needed also to permeate the educational, governmental and business institutions of the country.
>
> Our decision was to educate ourselves in the whole national situation. Right away we got into touch with the leaders of every part of the national life, and asked them to inform us. We called on the heads of the labour movement and of the National Chamber of Commerce and also the manufacturers. We went also to the heads of both the large farmers' association and the small farmers' group. We went to the leaders of each political party in the parliament, to the heads of the medical association and of the nurses.
>
> Little more than a year later there was a sudden invasion of the German army, navy and air force into both Denmark and Norway, taking them largely by surprise. Christian Harhoff, head of the Copenhagen Handelsbank, and a well-known shipowner, was one of the leaders of the group that had been formed during the six weeks campaign some months earlier. He realised that there would be a strict prohibition of meetings by the occupying forces, so he called up everyone of his group and all those who had been speakers during that series of evenings, inviting them to the Harhoffs' large apartment that very evening. Out of that meeting came initiatives that greatly helped to unite divided groups to stand and act together in the first difficult years of the occupation.[12]

Another group had already founded LAB, the National Movement to Combat Unemployment, led by Valdemar Hvidt, a

Supreme Court Lawyer. He and Colonel H.A.V. Hansen of the Danish Army worked intensively to persuade the government, the business community and the powerful labour movement to develop a plan. They started new businesses, such as bicycle parking-lots with mechanics to repair what was needed, as there was virtually no petrol and everyone rode to work on a bicycle. Since the demobilised army officers were without anything to do, Hansen and Hvidt through their organisations got them to divide the country up, county by county, and the officers went to every farm and business to find out what repairs and improvements could be done. In some cases the government provided low-cost loans, and the unions cooperated to make such work possible, so that hundreds of farms and businesses were made more serviceable. This initiative, besides creating employment, enabled farmers to raise thousands more pigs through the collection of waste food from homes. The employment programme deprived the occupation authorities of a case for transporting redundant workers to Germany.

Colonel Hansen, with another organisation, became the channel for uniting politicians and people with army officers under a single command in the resistance movement. Swift and clandestine operations by hundreds of Danes transported most of the Jews from Copenhagen and elsewhere to safety in Sweden — just as the Gestapo were moving to make a mass arrest.[13]

References

1. FB: 351

2. Schweitzer: 102

3. FB: 143-4, Mackinac, July 1943. For the four standards, see p. 20.

4. FB: 7 (note)

5. FB: 12, Kronborg, 9/6/35

6. FB: 160, Caux, 15/7/47

7. FB: 86, London, 1/1/39

8. FB: 15, Oxford, July 1935

9. FB: 19, New York, 20/11/35

10. FB: 351, 1937

11. Alan Thornhill: *One Fight More* (London 1972), 48ff

12. Howard Blake: *Way to Go* (Merrifield, Virginia, USA, 1992), 81-6

13. Henrik S. Nissen and Henning Poulsen: *På Dansk Friheds Grund (Foundations for Danish Freedom;* Gyldendal 1963), in cooperation with the Danish Ministry of Education, the Ministry of Cultural Affairs and the Carlsberg Foundation: 'About initiatives by people from the Oxford Group just before and during the German occupation of Denmark 1940-45'; *Folk og Forsvar gennem 25 år. Forsvarets Oplysnings- og Velfærdstjeneste 1966 (People and Defence through 25 years);* published by The Information and Educational Department of the Danish Defence, 1966). Information from Keld Jørgensen.

CHAPTER 9

THE FAMILY AND EDUCATION

In our day and age woes are coming, and many of these must be seen as the consequence of our departure, in so many ways, from the moral guidelines God has given mankind through His prophets and teachers. A most striking survey of this decline is to be found in Allan Bloom's *The Closing of the American Mind* (1988), as telling an indictment of our civilisation in Europe as it is of that in America. He points to the decay of the university as a key area in the matter of decadence, along with the decay of religion, an outcome of the decline of the family.

> Attending church or synagogue, praying at the table, were a way of life, inseparable from the moral education that was supposed to be the family's special responsibility in this democracy ... The things one was supposed to do ... were all incarnated in the Bible stories.

Science, having separated itself from Philosophy, marches on, producing ever more modern miracles, among them TV and the pill.

> Parents can no longer control the atmosphere of the home and have even lost the will to do so. With great subtlety and energy, television enters not only the room, but also the tastes of old and young alike, appealing to the immediately pleasant and subverting whatever does not conform to it.[1] (59) And with radio and TV and the now inevitable Walkman, rock music has come to dominate the lives of the young, with its one appeal only, a barbaric appeal, to sexual desire – not to

love, not *eros*, but sexual desire undeveloped and untutored ...
An enormous industry cultivates the taste for the orgiastic
state of feeling connected with sex ...(73)

Max Nordau's forecasts as the last century ended, about the
sexual aspects of decadence, have been direfully realised. He spoke
of the need for determined resistance (which has so far not been
adequate) against

the professional pornographists who ... poison the springs
whence flows the life of future generations. No task of
civilisation has been so painfully laborious as the subjugation
of lasciviousness. The pornographist would take from us the
fruit of this, the hardest struggle of humanity. To him we must
show no mercy.[2]

Frank Buchman said:

Take purity. You may say that it is just a personal matter. But
what is happening to the nation? ... Too few try to bring a
great cleansing force to the nation. What is going to happen to
a nation when nobody brings a cure any more? Broken homes,
unstable children, the decay of culture, the seeding plot of
revolution.[3]

Those engaged in education or the care of the young have a
major part in creating a new mental atmosphere.

Then family life ensures the nation's health, and prepares God-
governed children who are fit to be citizens. Then education
finds its inspiration as teachers and students, morally sane, are
taught by God.[4]

This is an art that everyone wants to learn, and heaven
help us if we don't learn it. We need to learn it for the sake of
our own children. Your own children must come and tell you
about themselves and you will share with them because you

know what a rascal you were yourself. That is the way to win your children, and that is the reason why this crowd of youth flocks around. They will go to a man who understands them, who doesn't talk too good or appear too wise, a man who shares.[5]

Compare also the role of universities:

We must get the new spirit through men. Universities hold a key position in bringing this about. The function of universities in a world crisis is to create new men who can fashion the new civilisation.[6]

In 'The Making of a Miracle' Buchman describes his 'laboratory time' at Pennsylvania State College, where — at the time of his arrival — 'the life of the students reflected the godlessness of the place. The first night I got there, there were nineteen liquor parties.'[7] Part of the miracle was the change in Bill Pickle, *alias* Gilliland, whose position as a college janitor enabled him to supply the liquor for the students. As Secretary of the YMCA Buchman revitalised its sphere of activity with a new programme of classes and meetings. According to the college chaplain, 'he seemed to be going among people constantly. Every day you would see him walking on the campus with one of the fellows, chatting and laughing.'[8]

The change in Gilliland dealt with the problem of alcoholism.

I have seen real catastrophe in the lives of students, and I say, very sincerely and very bluntly, it's a hell of a life if you don't have the Gospel of Jesus Christ. There is only one thing which is adequate and it is someone who can change you, someone who loves you. If you have this power, men and women will come to you night and day for an answer. All sorts of people.[9]

Buchman started his work at 'Penn State' in 1909. The previous year had seen the remarkable response at Oxford to the visit of John R. Mott, Buchman's major sponsor at the college. This response to Mott, and eventually to Buchman at Penn State, was typical of the 'campus movement'. Then the Great War intervened. This was a disaster not only in the ghastly casualties, destruction and disease which it caused, but also in 'the frightful moral collapse' noted by Mott.[10] Thereafter Mott concentrated his efforts on building up the ecumenical movement, while his younger associate took over the torch which he relinquished.

When Buchman came to Oxford in 1921 he was, to some extent, swimming against the tide.

> Unheralded and unknown, one by one he met people and made friends. He loved and understood that sceptical, restless, war-scarred generation. He listened to their theories about life and told them true stories about people. He answered arguments with experience. Some of the leading undergraduates of the University gathered around him. Many who had been problems to the authorities became pioneers in a new spirit. Prayer was publicly offered from a University pulpit giving thanks for the illumination which had come to Oxford.[11]

> He held no official position in Oxford. He gave no lectures, had founded no society, was not at that time identified with any movement. He was just a man who appeared from time to time and got to know people. He had friends among the intellectuals and the athletes, the drunks and the dons, the pious and the popular. He also got to know people in a deeper

sense. He would stay as a guest in a college, or rent some lodgings, and very soon there would be a chain of visitors knocking at his door. Some came bristling for an argument, some came weighed down by a private worry or a hidden fear. Some were just curious or bored with a life that was too small.[12]

The Roman Catholic Bishop Emeritus of Leeds, William Gordon Wheeler, looking back sixty years in an address at Evensong in University College, Oxford, said:

> The Oxford Group under the able leadership of Frank Buchman and Professor Grensted took Oxford by storm ... Against a background of the hunger marchers and general malaise in the country, the spiritual quality of the Group motivated some of the finest young men and women of that generation ... The simple challenge of the four absolutes and the factor of guidance set many free ... That spiritual movement of the Holy Spirit which was active here in my day is still at it, effectively, in the work of reconciliation and of Moral Re-Armament, against the current breakdown of social relations where alcoholism, violence and consumerism threaten to tear God out of the human heart.[13]

Changes in the faculty could have revolutionary results. When, at the University of Rhodesia, Professor Desmond Reader decided to apologise to an African colleague for treating him as a lightweight, he opened the way for fruitful talks between members of the white establishment in the country and African nationalists – people who had never met each other before – which paved the way for the 'cabinet of conscience', the ending of the civil war and the creation of Zimbabwe.[14]

In Switzerland, the challenge that came in a time of quiet to Theophil Spoerri, Professor of French and Italian Literature at the University of Zurich, was to 'come down from the second floor', his ivory tower where he could hide away from everything that disturbed him or his work. Coming down from the top of his tall house not only improved his communication with his wife (as his children soon noticed) but with people in general, as they became more important than books. Not that his literary or university work suffered — his books on Pascal and Dante gained him a European reputation, and he became Rector of the University — but his outreach to his fellow-citizens and involvement in wider responsibilities led him to initiate the *Gotthardbund* (League of Gotthard), when war engulfed Europe in 1939. Its aim, successfully achieved, was to counter defeatism and ideological infiltration during the years when Switzerland was surrounded by potentially hostile armies.[15]

References

1. RCM: 268. Quotations from Bloom with page references.

2. *Degeneration*, 556-7

3. FB: 143

4. FB: 65, Interlaken, 10/9/38

5. FB: 337, California, June 1948

6. FB: 93, Oglethorpe University, June 1939

7. FB: 330, California, June 1948

8. Lean, 34

9. FB: 337

10. Mott: *Addresses and Papers* III, 579; RCM:152

11. FB: xiii

12. Alan Thornhill: *Best of Friends* (London 1986), 64

13. 31/1/93; Canon Grensted was Nolloth Professor of the Philosophy of the Christian Religion at the University of Oxford

14. Hugh P. Elliott: *Darkness and Dawn in Zimbabwe* (London 1978), 19ff; Alec Smith: *Now I call him Brother* (Basingstoke 1984), 72 ff

15. John Lester and Pierre Spoerri: *Rediscovering Freedom* (London 1992), 24; Theophil Spoerri: *Dynamic out of Silence*, Foreword by Garth Lean (London 1976)

CHAPTER 10

STRATEGY

Listening to God and surrender to Him, these are steps which follow what Buchman calls 'an initial enlistment' of those 'who have yet to learn the discipline to make the answer effective in these fateful days.'[1] Elsewhere Buchman compares the step of surrender to God to 'a deed, like the transfer of property, so you turn over your life to God, for full and complete direction as a fellow-revolutionary.'[2] In his own experience, the decisive moment for Buchman came during his time at Pennsylvania State College, when he 'decided to give his will, as distinct from his life in general, to God,'[3] following another decision to give at least an hour to a 'quiet time' in the early morning each day.

Streeter wrote:

> Once we realise ... that the only sensible course for the individual is to ask what is God's plan for him ... common sense demands that we give ourselves entirely to it. At first sight the suggestion that a man should make a complete surrender — I would prefer the word dedication — of his will to God, sounds like an invitation to throw away that essential freedom and spontaneity which constitutes the fine essence of human personality. But this is yet another fallacy of the imagination. Admittedly, to make a complete surrender of one's will to any fellow human being is a renunciation of liberty; but God is not another human being. He is the all-pervading Reality; 'in Him', as Paul says, 'we live, and move,

and have our being.' And it is the testimony of great souls in the past, and present, who have tried the way of surrendering their will to Him, that His 'service is perfect freedom' and that 'in His will is our peace.'

In life as actually experienced examples may be found of a self-surrender which is at the same time the highest form of self-realisation. The members of an orchestra renounce nothing of their liberty when they take the lead from the conductor. Indeed, the greater the conductor the higher is the degree of spontaneity evoked by him; and the more completely each performer surrenders himself to the conductor's lead, the more completely does he realise, and know that he is realising, his own individual potentialities and powers. Hence the ovation sometimes given by an orchestra to its leader at the end of a great piece greatly rendered. A living experience like this affords an analogy which goes deeper than mere metaphor to that harmony between human and divine will which is a personal experience to religious men, but of which the nature necessarily eludes explanation in terms of abstract reasoning.

God being God, and His plan being my highest good, it is not slavery but liberty to conform my will to His.[4]

Giving adequate time to listening to God is basic in Frank Buchman's thinking. 'Disciplined direction' of the mind makes possible 'direct messages from the Mind of God to the mind of man'[5] – we can then 'learn the great compelling truth, the great symphony'.[6] In the words of Alphonse Gratry, vanquishing 'the inner talkativeness of empty thoughts, of restless desires and entrenched prejudices', we can take our pen (or biro) and 'write for God and ourselves. When the soul meditates quietly and hears something from God, peace and joy flood in.'[7]

Truths revealed in silence; the answer to the lies and unreality on which so much of warped human society is based – 'the inhuman power of the lie', as Pasternak calls it[8] – not only in the Russia which he depicted, but also in the constant 'pressure to co-operate with small lies' in the West.[9] Solzhenitsyn proclaims the same message of silence when he writes of a character in *Cancer Ward*:

> His inner self demanded silent contemplation, free of external sounds, conversations, thought of work, free of everything that made him a doctor. Particularly after the death of his wife, inner consciousness had seemed to crave a pure transparency. It was just this sort of silent immobility, without planned or even floating thoughts, which gave him a sense of purity and fulfilment. At such moments an image of the whole meaning of existence ... was conjured up in his mind ...'[10]

The pioneers of a new era – almost 'a new species of humanity', as Bergson calls them[11] – operate with a sense of strategy. At the dawn of Christianity St. Paul showed this sense, which took him throughout the eastern Empire and eventually to Rome. For these pioneers, spearheading moves towards a future of hope, strategy is not merely man-devised. Through taking time for God or 'the inner voice' we may perceive what we should do, how to work and inspire others. Laurens van der Post says that taking part in the 'main thrust towards the creation of a new kind of individual' involves an experience as of listening to an inner voice; absolute obedience to this brings 'a feeling of happiness almost too keen to endure.'[12]

In Buchman's words,

Divine guidance must become the normal experience of ordinary men and women. Any man can pick up divine messages if he will put his receiving set in order. This is normal prayer.[13]

There are questions to ask oneself and practical points to consider in listening to God.

Guidance is when we are in communication with God. The first step in re-orienting our minds to God is to listen twice as much as we talk. This is a simple programme of how to begin. Yet here lies the strategy to win the world from her egocentric ways. For immediately self is the centre of the picture, there war has begun, whether in individuals or nations. Fear is another kind of guidance. People are afraid, and so they will not fight the daily battle against selfishness.[14]

Everyone is guided by something. What are you guided by? Is it your own desires? Is it your pocket-book? Your fears? Your wife? Your husband? Or what the neighbours think? If it is your own selfish plan, you are an enemy of the nation.[15]

From trying to listen to God occasionally, we may go on to 'form a daily habit.'[16]

It is only necessary to obey the rules. The first rule is that we listen honestly for everything that may come – and if we are wise we write it down. The second rule is that we test the thoughts that come, to see which are from God. One test is the Bible. It is steeped in the experience through the centuries of men who have dared, under Divine revelation, to live experimentally with God. There, culminating in the life of Jesus Christ, we find the highest moral and spiritual challenge – complete honesty, purity, unselfishness and love.

Another spiritual test is, 'What do others say who also listen to God?' This is an unwritten law of fellowship. It is also an acid test of one's commitment to God's plan.[17]

According to B.H. Streeter, religion was 'Power' or it was virtually nothing; and Power would come from 'the conviction of sin which this age requires'. And as for 'sharing', Streeter considered it both a spiritual and psychological necessity – finding 'the right person to whom to confide painful incidents of maturer years – the moral failures ...' In this way it becomes possible for a person, after speaking 'clearly and fully' about some shameful or painful incident in the past, 'to put behind him both the memory and the emotions associated with it, and, as it were, permanently to detach himself.'[18]

Frank Buchman has described his own experience of change, from a condition of defeat and futility. 'I was personally at war. An experience of the Cross made me a new type of revolutionary.'[19]

Ambition, with consequent resentment at his plans being frustrated by others, had sapped his spiritual power.

> The first serious crisis came in Frank's life when a fellow-student at Mount Airy Seminary, Philadelphia, accused him of ambition. This accusation smote him severely, and he chose the most difficult quarter of Philadelphia for his initial labours.[20]

But he found the accusation true.

> My work had become my idol. I had difficulties with my Board. We got up against each other and it was then that I learnt that I too, like those children, wanted to have my own way, and that the solution of our social problems lay in the human heart.[21]

He described his experience of change at the Keswick Convention of 1908:

A tiny village church ... the speaker – a woman ... [Her] simple talk personalised the Cross for me that day, and suddenly I had a poignant vision of the Crucified. There was infinite suffering on the face of the Master, and I realised for the first time the great abyss separating myself from Him. That was all. But it produced in me a vibrant feeling, as though a strong current of life had suddenly been poured into me, and afterwards a dazed sense of a great spiritual shaking-up. There was no longer the feeling of a divided will, no sense of calculation and argument, of oppression and helplessness; a wave of strong emotion, following the will to surrender, rose up within me from the depths of an estranged spiritual life, and seemed to lift my soul from its anchorage of selfishness, bearing it across that great sundering abyss to the foot of the Cross. With this deeper experience of how the love of God had bridged the chasm dividing me from Him, and the new sense of buoyant life that had come, I returned to the house feeling a powerful urge to share my experience.[22]

He wrote letters of apology to each member of the Board for nurturing ill-will against them. Another experience followed – a young man, son of the family with whom he was staying, asked him to tell him about his new experience, and himself decided to surrender his will to God.[23]

Some sincere Christians have wondered how Buchman could return again and again to his Keswick experience, and at the same time help men like U Nu and Abdel Khalek Hassouna in their personal and public lives without demanding that they join the Christian Church. It was certainly not because his faith in or dependence on Christ lessened with the years – quite the contrary.

The key seems to have been that Buchman was dedicated

to help the people he met to take the next step which God was revealing to them. His friends of other religions knew what he believed and what he tried to live — and were attracted by it. He respected their sincere beliefs, and knew that they had often absorbed a distorted idea of Christianity from the way they had seen people from so-called Christian countries live. He saw his part as demonstrating the beauty and relevance of Christ's living presence in a person or a community — and leaving the Holy Spirit room to work in their hearts as He wished. He was sure that God could make His will known to anyone, just as He did to the Jews in the Old Testament, and that He did not enquire first whether the person seeking Him was a Christian, a person of some different faith or, like the Ruhr Communists, of no faith at all. So, in the deepest sense, he did not aspire to proselytize, but to put people in touch with the Spirit which 'blows where it likes'.

So, with U Nu, he concentrated on helping him to believe he could receive guidance. To the Ghanaian Muslim leader, the Tolon Na, he had simply remarked, 'When did you last steal?' When he emerged, still a good Muslim, from the violent reappraisal of his life into which this one remark had pitched him, the Tolon Na had put right everything in his life which he could see that he had done wrong. He often explained that the Cross meant to him that when God's will crossed his will, he must choose God's will.[24]

Restitution, guidance, life-changing, are part of the experience of change, and its fruit.

This applies to the spiritual statesmen and pioneers world-wide. All the great spiritual leaders have played their part in preparing the way for the forward moves of mankind. They prepared the consciousness of mankind for the present moment in history, because today all the streams of history are flowing together. It is a change on the level of ideas, but accompanied by a change in the way of life. This is the leaven which has been at work all down the ages changing the nature of the world.

It is a message of hope for everyone around the globe, making possible the dawn of a new age. As the drift into decadence continues, we can either live according to norms which have become debased, or we can pioneer the new civilisation and another flowering of the human spirit.

References

1. FB: 120, USA, 2/12/39

2. FB: 58, Visby, 16/8/38

3. FB: Lean, 36, 74

4. BHS: 13

5. FB: 131, USA, 4/6/40

6. FB: 72, London, 11/11/38

7. *Decline and Renewal*, 257-8

8. Boris Pasternak: *Dr Zhivago* (London 1958), 453

9. 'For a Change,' April 1990, John Lester: 'In my view.'

10. A. Solzhenitsyn: *Cancer Ward* (Harmondsworth 1971), 459-60

11. Henri Bergson: *The two Sources of Morality and Religion* (London 1935), 77

12. *A Walk with a White Bushman*, 82, 140, 144

13. FB: 12, Kronborg, 9/6/35

14. FB: 112, USA, 29/10/39

15. FB: 39, London, 9/8/36

16. FB: 72, London, 11/11/38 (see also 338)

17. FB: 36, Birmingham, 9/8/36

18. *Reality*, 255n., 256

19. FB: 113, USA, 29/10/39

20. FB: 313-4. Quoted from A.J. Russell: *For Sinners Only* (London 1932), 55. See also Lean, 30ff, 12

21. FB: 83, London, November 1938

22. FB: 314-5; Russell, 57-9. The speaker was Mrs Jessie Penn-Lewis (see Lean, 30 and M.O. Guldseth: *Streams* (Fritz Creek, Alaska, 1982), 64-6, 84).

23. FB: 187

24. Lean, 513

BIOGRAPHICAL NOTES

(Reference to Chambers Encyclopaedia is to the 1908 edition)

Adenauer, Konrad (1876-1967). For many years Burgomeister (Lord Mayor) of Cologne until dismissed by Hitler. After World War II Chairman of Christian-Democrat Party in British-occupied Zone. Chancellor of German Federal Republic 1949-63. Policies of cooperation with West European states and USA, culminating in the launch of the European Community of Coal and Steel (1950). Supported its development with the Common Market and Euratom (Treaty of Rome, 1957).

Arnold, Matthew (1822-88). Poet, critic, Inspector of schools, Professor of Poetry at Oxford.

Arnold, Thomas (1795-1842). Headmaster of Rugby School (1828-41). He had published three volumes of his *History of Rome* before his untimely death, a year after being appointed Regius Professor of Modern History at Oxford.

Barth, Karl (1886-1968) His *Epistle to Romans* brought him to prominence as a theologian in 1919. At the time of Hitler's attempt to take over the German Evangelical Church, many clergy were prepared to compromise, but others were encouraged by Barth's resounding 'NO! to both the spirit and the letter of this doctrine' in his book *Theologische Existenz heute!* (1933). Held Chair of Theology from 1930 at Bonn, but left for Basle (his birthplace) under Nazi pressure. Championed reconciliation of Germany with war-time enemies, lecturing in ruins of Bonn University 1946 and 1947.

Bergson, Henri (1859-1941). French philosopher.

Bonhoeffer, Dietrich (1906-45). Theologian. Carried out a remarkable ministry especially among young people, in one of the poorest districts of Berlin, then became Chaplain of the Evangelical Church at Barcelona, Spain (1928) and Sydenham, London (1933-5). A founder of the Confessing Church in opposition to the Protestant Reich Church under Hitler's supporters. Directed an illegal seminary for ordinands on principles presented in his books *Life Together* and *The Cost of Discipleship*. Joined the Abwehr (the German army's intelligence and counter-espionage service), and with near relatives and others became part of a dissident network. Imprisoned April 1943 until his execution in April 1945. *Letters and Papers from Prison* were published after the war (1953).

Bright, John (1811-89) Leading member of (British) Anti-Corn Law League and promoter of free trade. M.P., President of Board of Trade 1868-70. Warm supporter of Abraham Lincoln.

Buchman, Frank N.D. (1878-1961). Studied theology and arts subjects at Muhlenberg College, Pennsylvania, graduating (1902) at Mount Airy Seminary, Philadelphia. Minister of a new church in a poor part of Philadelphia, where he founded and managed a hospice for young men (1904). Resigned after a dispute with the committee which provided part of the finance while opposing his standards of care and provision (1907). A Christian experience at the Keswick Convention in England (1908) healed his bitterness and re-oriented his life. YMCA Secretary at Penn State College (1909-16). Lecturer at Hartford Theological Seminary, Connecticut (1916-22) during which period he went on missions to India, China and Japan. He then began to train a nucleus of committed people, mainly at Princeton University and Oxford. As the work grew, he took a team to South Africa, where it was named the Oxford Group, and to many other countries. As war loomed in 1938 he called for 'moral and spiritual re-armament', hence the name Moral Re-Armament (MRA). For his work of reconciliation he was decorated by the governments of France, Germany and Japan.

Burckhardt, Jakob (1818-97). Historian. Another of his books is *The Age of Constantine the Great* (1863).

Chouraqui, André (b. 1917) originates from Algeria, where his family had been established for several centuries, since being expelled from Spain. French educated, with a doctorate in Law (in addition Hebrew and Judaic study), he was deprived of his French citizenship and his right to follow his profession by the Vichy government on account of being

Jewish. Fought in the Maquis in a unit which spent its off-duty time studying the Bible in the original languages. Having previously lost his faith, his conversion had come through Catholics and Protestants, and also through Muslims whom he got to know in the Sahara region – he writes of 'the shock of my discovery of God by way of Christian and Muslim spirituality'. After practising as a judge in post-war Algeria, he migrated to Israel where for a time he was Deputy Mayor of Jerusalem. He declined the offer of the presidency of Israel in order to devote himself, besides other writing, to the translation into French of the Bible, both Old and New Testaments, from the original languages, and to producing an illustrated encyclopaedia, *L'Univers de la Bible*. His name as a writer was made in France soon after the Six-day War of 1967 with his *Lettre à un ami arabe*. His most recent works are an autobiography, *L'Amour fort comme la mort* and a translation into French of the Koran.

Constantine I, the Great (?280-337). Roman Emperor 306-37. Succeeded his father, Constantius I; ruled jointly with Licinius until 324. By Edict of Milan (313) Christianity was given recognised status and supported by him. Presided at the Church Council of Nicaea; moved capital to new city of Constantinople; ended inflation by stabilising the gold solidus.

Drummond, Henry (1851-97). While a student he helped Moody on his mission to Britain, 1873-5. Lecturer, and later Professor of Natural Science, at Free Church College, Glasgow. As a teacher and through his writings he expressed Christian ideals in the still novel doctrine of evolution and of his own scientific findings. Capacity-filled weekly meetings for students. World-wide travels, including the USA, where he helped Moody on campuses and inspired him to hold summer conferences at Northfield. Best-known books: *The Ascent of Man* and *The Greatest Thing in the World*.

Fox, George (1624-91). Founded the Society of Friends (Quakers). '"The inward light' was the central idea of his teaching ... He was not only a great religious, but a great social reformer." (Chambers Encyclopaedia).

Gandhi, Mohandas Karamchand (1869-1948). Indian political and religious leader, known as Mahatma (great soul). After practising as lawyer in South Africa took on leadership (with the Congress Party) for independence of India from Britain. Asserted Hindu ethics by teaching scriptures and by abstemious life, spinning cotton and encouraging economic self-sufficiency, in his ashram (place of retreat); also by his non-violent passive resistance to British rule, which brought him periods of imprisonment. Participated in conferences with the British for the transition to independence. Assassinated by Hindu fanatic.

Gasperi, Alcide De (1881-1954). Survived Fascist persecution as librarian in the Vatican. Leader of Christian-Democratic Party and Prime Minister of Italy 1945-53.

Gratry, Alphonse (1805-72). Director of Collège St. Stanislas 1840-7. Chaplain of the École Normale 1847-52. Joined the contemplative and teaching Oratorians and revitalised the Oratory in France 1852-69.

Gregory I, The Great (?550-604) Member of a professional Roman family. Resigned office of Praetor of Rome to enter one of several monasteries which he founded. Nuncio (ambassador) at Constantinople for three years; on return acclaimed Pope by the people of Rome (590). A great administrator and reformer, he ensured food supplies for the city, negotiated with Lombard invaders, regulated Church ritual and music, trained the clergy and suppressed corruption. 'Was most gentle in his treatment of heathens and Jews, and he used all his efforts to repress slave-dealing and to mitigate the severity of slavery.' (Chambers Encyclopaedia).

Hansen, Hans A.V., Lt-Col. (1881-1948). Met Oxford Group (Moral-Re-Armament) in 1935, which became of decisive significance for his life. Initiated the work of 'Folk og Værn' (The Danish People and the Armed Forces). 'The 9th of April [1940; date of German occupation of Denmark] struck him to the heart. But he possessed a Christian faith and a will inspired by that faith, so he was invincible. Forthwith he came to grips with the situation and began to instil faith and courage into those around him. He worked to recreate harmony within the forces and to create understanding among the people for the task of the Army, by fostering the spirit which does not blame others but accepts personal responsibility and fights for the whole situation.' (Major-General E.C.V. Møller, Chief of the General Staff.)

Harnack, Adolf von (1851-1930). From 1888 Professor of Church History at Berlin University.

Hassouna, Abdel-Khalek (1898-1992). Degrees in Law, Economics and Political Science at Universities of Cairo and Cambridge. Governor of Alexandria in 1942, when, with many people fleeing the city during Rommel's advance, his broadcasts stabilised a situation of panic. Minister successively of Social Affairs, Education, and Foreign Affairs. Appointed Secretary-General of the Arab League in 1952, reappointed for three more 5-year terms. 'In 1958, when events in Lebanon brought the world to the brink of war ... he painstakingly bridged the gulf of bitter division between Arab opinion behind which the Great Powers had ranged themselves in hostile confrontation ... A united Arab resolution eventually emerged and the General Assembly [of the U.N.] passed it unanimously ... He modestly attributed the result to his personal faith, which he linked with his long association with Moral Re-Armament and which sustained him, he said, in the most difficult affairs of modern life.' (*The Times*, 23/1/92).

Hvidt, Valdemar (1897-1986). Danish lawyer: High Court (1927); Supreme Court (1937); Chairman of LAB (the National Association for Combatting Unemployment, 1939-56). 'A stone that is too heavy to carry can be carried away when it is divided into smaller pieces' was the motto he gave which inspired the LAB campaign of visiting all the towns and villages of Denmark.

John Paul II, Karol Wojtyla (b. 1920). First Pole to be elected Pope (1978) and first non-Italian Pope in 450 years. His visits to Poland while still under Communist rule (1979, 1983) inspired mass support for the Solidarity movement, moving not only Poland but also other countries of Central and Eastern Europe towards independence. A man of 'scintillating talent and profound spirituality.'

Kierkegaard, Søren (1813-55). Danish philosopher, who applied the Socratic method to the fundamental principles of Christianity. 'In dialectical skill, eloquence, and imaginative qualities he is scarcely inferior to Plato.' (Chambers Encyclopaedia).

Lacordaire, Jean (1802-61). French theologian and preacher. Contributed to the periodical of de Lamennais, *l'Avenir*, until it was condemned by Pope Gregory XVI. Made his name with highly popular *Conférences de Notre-Dame de Paris*.

Lamennais, Félicité de (1782-1854). 'Inspired much of the political thought of the 19th and 20th centuries ... a forerunner of religious modernism ...' (Chambers Encyclopaedia 1967). His *Essai sur l'indifférence en matière de religion* and *Paroles d'un croyant* proclaimed political freedom to be the essence of Catholic Christianity as viewed in a wide ecumenical context. Elected to the National Assembly (Parliament) in 1848.

Lecky, William E.H. (1838-1903). Irish historian, M.P. Best known works: *History of European Morals from Augustine to Charlemagne, History of England in the Eighteenth Century* (8 vols.).

Lincoln, Abraham (1809-1865). Ancestors from England 1638. Educated in 'backwoods schools', but mostly self-educated, after farm-work and logging. As a village postmaster studied law and grammar. Became a lawyer. Represented Illinois as founding member of Republican Party (1856) opposing the extension of slavery in USA. Elected President 1860. Pro-slavery leaders attacked Fort Sumter (Charleston), starting the civil war (1861). After election to a second term and the ending of the war, he was assassinated.

Moltke, Helmuth von (1907-45). Great-nephew of the 19th century Prussian general of the same name; had inherited his estate and title (Graf = Count). English mother. Specialist in international law. As a member of the Abwehr (see under 'Bonhoeffer') during World War II, he used his position to protect Jews and other persecuted people. Warned the Jews of Denmark of imminent danger of deportation (October 1943), making their rescue possible. His 'circle', meeting on his estate at Kreisau, became part of the network for replacing Nazism by a democratic regime. The government of the [future] Germany sees in Christianity the foundation for the moral and religious renewal of our people, for the surmounting of hate and lies, for the rebuilding of the European Community of peoples.'

Monnet, Jean (1888-1979). Organised co-operation in supply matters between France, Britain and other allies in both World Wars. Deputy Secretary-General of League of Nations after World War I. Having supported General de Gaulle in World War II, he was put in charge of the commissariat for the modernisation and re-equipment of French industry and agriculture (1946). He worked out the Plan for administering jointly the production and distribution of coal and steel by France, West Germany and other countries in the European Coal and Steel Community – as the Schuman Plan it was launched by Robert Schuman, the Foreign Minister of France (1950). Monnet was in charge of the ECSC 1951-55, then Chairman of the Action Committee for the United States of Europe.

Moody, Dwight L. (1837-99). Descended from a family which was among the earliest settlers (1630's) in Connecticut. As a young businessman he started a Bible class for the waifs of the Chicago streets. The response was such that he gave up a promising career to continue this work full-time. He launched out into campaigns in partnership with I.D. Sankey who provided a distinctive musical element. The first great enterprise of the two men was the mission of 1873-5 in Britain, followed by another (1883). Main centre of their work was on Moody's estate at Northfield, Massachusetts, where many students, including Frank Buchman, attended conferences and found their calling in various walks of life. Another was Robert Speer, who in his book *The Principles of Jesus* set forth the four 'absolute standards of Jesus ... No man who through the deliberate act of surrender of the human will to absolute standards of purity, honesty, unselfishness and love, has once felt the coursing of these immortal powers in his spirit, can ever after find any experience of this new life tame or commonplace.'

Mott, John R. (1865-1955) Student leader in YMCA at Cornell University, known for his 'individual work with individuals as the real power through which decisive, life-changing work of a permanent character was to be done.' In charge of all student work in North America under YMCA auspices. Attended Moody's summer conference 1886, from which came the Student Volunteer Movement. Chaired the World Missionary Conference, Edinburgh 1910. He envisaged action at what he called this 'decisive hour of the world's history' which would lead to 'the enthroning of Christ in the individual life, in social life, in international life, in international relations, in every relationship of mankind.' His ecumenical work bore fruit in the World Council of Churches.

Niemöller, Martin (1892-1984). U-Boat Commander in World War I. Founded Pastors Emergency League (Pfarrernotbund) 1933, in opposition to Hitler's policy of putting 'German Christians' (pro-Nazi) in control of the German Evangelical Church. One of the founders of the Confessing Church, proclaimed at the Synod of Barmen, 1934. Arrested (Dachau and other camps). Took a leading part in rebuilding the German Evangelical Church after the war, and in reconciliation with former enemies through the 'Stuttgart Confession of Guilt', 1945.

Nietzsche, Friedrich (1844-1900). German Philosopher. *Thus spake Zarathustra* and other works. Regarded moral laws as a remnant of Christian superstition. His ideal was the superman, with the 'will to power'.

Nordau, Max (1849-1923). Studied medicine at Budapest, travelled widely in Europe, settled as a doctor in Hungary, then Paris. Besides *Degeneration* (1893), published *Conventional Lies of Society,* and *Paradoxes,* also novels, plays and poems.

Penn, William (1644-1718). As an Oxford student was converted to Quakerism. His father, Admiral William Penn, had close connections with the royal family, which he continued, and this saved him from some of the more extreme penalties resulting from his beliefs and behaviour. With the support of Charles II founded the colony of Pennsylvania in America (1682), developing good relations with the 'Indian' tribes.

Post, Sir Laurence van der (b. 1906, South Africa). Farmer, soldier, explorer, conservationist, and a prolific writer: many books on Africa. Has also written on Japan and Russia. *The Seed and the Sower* (1963) was filmed as 'Merry Christmas, Mr Lawrence,' dealing with his time as a prisoner of war with the Japanese.

Proudhon, Pierre Joseph (1809-65). French socialist thinker. His most famous book, *Qu'est ce que la propriété?* (1840) became notorious for its short answer 'Property is theft'. Was elected to the Assembly (Parliament) during the revolutionary year 1848, but the violence of his utterances led to his imprisonment. A self-taught, learned scholar, he wrote among other books *Système des contradictions économiques*.

Rees-Mogg, Baron William (b. 1928). Editor of *The Times* 1967-81; editorial positions on other papers. Vice-Chairman of Board of Governors of BBC, and chairmanships in the arts, journalism and finance. Business consultant. Author.

Schweitzer, Albert (1875-1965). Born and lived early life in Alsace where he was Principal of a theological college (1903-6). Well-known organist and musicologist (book on Bach). Philosopher ('reverence for life') and theologian (*The Quest of the Historical Jesus,* 1910). After training as medical doctor, founded, built and worked in hospital at Lambaréné, Gabon (French Equatorial Africa), described in *On the Edge of the Primeval Forest* (1922) and other books.

Shaftesbury, Earl of (Anthony Ashley Cooper, 1801-85). 'From the early training of a faithful old servant, Maria Millis, the future philanthropist received his earliest and deepest religious impressions.' (Chambers Encyclopaedia). First-Class Classics, Oxford. Member of House of Commons 1826-51, then succeeded father in House of Lords. Promoted bills for the better treatment of lunatics, for abolishing employment of boy chimney-sweeps, for restricting employment of women and young persons (the Ten Hours' Bill), another for excluding them from work in coal mines, and for regulating conditions in factories and workshops. 'Relinquishing society and all amusements, he gave his life to other beneficent schemes, and his time and strength were exhausted by letters, interviews, chairmanships, and speeches.' (Chambers Encyc.)

89

Shibusawa, Eiichi, Viscount (1840-1931). From a peasant background, became a leading member of the government which modernised Japan after the Shogunate was overthrown under Emperor Meiji, putting the regime on a firm financial basis (1869). Became president of the First National Bank, which he helped to found (1873). He was 'involved in almost every enterprise associated with Japan's industrial development in this period. He retired in 1916 to devote himself to social welfare causes in which he continued active until his death aged 91.' (Encyclopaedia Britannica, 1985).

Solzhenitsyn, Alexandr (b. 1918). Russian novelist and historian, served in World War II, followed by eight years' imprisonment for criticising Stalin in a letter. Made his name with *One Day in the Life of Ivan Denisovich* (1962), based on his experiences in a forced-labour camp. Later writings, notably *The First Circle* and *Cancer Ward*, were refused publication by Soviet censorship, and were circulated covertly by so-called self-publishing (*samizdat*) and were also published abroad. After part of *The Gulag Archipelago* had been published in Paris he was exiled, and now lives in America.

Spaak, Paul Henri (1899-1972). As Prime Minister and Foreign Minister of Belgium during periods before and after World War II, he worked tirelessly for European union, especially in preparing the Treaty of Rome (1957).

Streeter, Burnett Hillman (1874-1937). Biblical scholar, theologian, philosopher. Canon of Hereford Cathedral. Fellow and (1933) Provost of the Queen's College, Oxford. One of six young Fellows and Chaplains who contributed essays to *Foundations* (1912), his being 'The historic Christ'. *The Four Gospels* became standard reading for scholars and students until now. Of *Reality* (1926) a reader commented, 'This has proved to me that those who believe in God do more thinking than those who do not.' Other books: *The Sadhu* [Sundar Singh] (1921); *Adventure* (with other contributors, 1927); *The Buddha and the Christ* (1932). 'His annual spring conference held at Old Jordans in Buckinghamshire revealed ... the extent and depth of his knowledge and learning.' (Arthur Burrell in *The Queen's College Record*, Vol. 6, Dec. 1987.)

Sun Yat-sen (1866-1925). First President of Republic of China, 1912. Organised Kuomintang Party. During the anarchic period in China coinciding with World War I and its aftermath, Sun attempted to establish a government for the country from his base at Canton.

Tolon Na, Alhadji Yakuba Tali, the (1896-1986). After some years teaching, he succeeded his father as Chief of the Tolon District, Northern Ghana. President of the Northern Territories Council. Member of Parliament and Speaker. High Commissioner (Ambassador) to Nigeria 1965-9, then Ambassador to Yugoslavia, Sierra Leone and Guinea. At Caux in 1954, one of his African colleagues was making a speech about the cost of dishonesty to a nation. Buchman turned with a smile to the Tolon Na and in an aside said, 'When did you last steal?' 'This struck me like a depth charge,' he afterwards wrote. 'I thought and thought. At last relief came when I decided to write down the number of times that I had stolen since my infancy. I made a note to return all textbooks I had brought home from the schools in which I taught: I also noted all the persons to whom I owed apologies.'

U Nu (b. 1901). Student leader in the independence movement at the University of Rangoon. Prime Minister of Burma 1948-58 and 1960-2. Imprisoned after coup by General Ne Win, then exiled, returning in 1980 to become a Buddhist monk.

Wesley, John (1703-91). Preacher, administrator, scholar. After his conversion experience in 1738, being denied usually the opportunity of preaching in churches, he followed Whitefield in open-air preaching, regularly at five a.m., having risen at four, to crowds which might be as large as 20,000 or even 30,000. During fifty years he travelled 250,000 miles, mostly on horseback, and preached 40,000 sermons. One of the greatest of hymn-writers (as was his brother Charles), he also wrote numerous books, including grammars of English, French, Latin, Greek and Hebrew, an English dictionary, histories of Rome, England, and the Church from earliest times – many of his writings and handbooks being designed for the itinerant preachers whom he trained or inspired. He gave away during his lifetime to charity all the money accruing from sales of these books, £30,000, a huge sum in present-day currency.

Wilberforce, William (1759-1833). M.P. for Hull and Yorkshire. In 1788 began campaign for abolition of slave trade. Abolition Bill passed in Parliament 1807. Continued with campaign for abolition of slavery in the British Empire. Published (1797) *A Practical View of the Prevailing Religious System of Professed Christians in the Higher and Middle Classes of the Country, Contrasted with Real Christianity.* He and his friends regarded themselves as 'part of a large united family', living in each other's homes. In their campaigning to abolish the slave trade and eventually slavery itself, and in promoting other notable reforms – including Wilberforce's great aim of reviving Christian morals and manners throughout the land – 'they assembled as frequently as possible to breakfast at each other's houses, or to discuss plans far into the night.' They worked together on documents and evidence, making out their case for presentation in Parliament or publication in various forms, and in so doing pioneered modern methods of propaganda with pamphlets, lectures, press articles and posters, with meetings and anniversaries, societies and subscriptions, and with a strategy for preparing petitions with thousands of signatures to bring public opinion to bear on the authorities at critical moments. In these campaigns women took a major part, opening the way to their eventual full participation in public life.

Wurm, Theophil (1868-1953). Bishop of Württemberg. He wrote: 'In Moral Re-Armament people do not talk so much about the Cross of Christ, but they live by the power of the Cross of Christ. All come under its influence. That is why they can unite people of different parties, nations and confessions.' (FB, 176)